12 Competitive Games and and Training Exercises

NICOLA PICA

Library of Congress Cataloging - in - Publication Data

Pica, Nicola
120 Competitive Games and Training Exercises

Original Title "Un gioco e via"
   Published by Ediaioni Nuova Prhomos

ISBN No. 1-890946-29-X
Library of Congress Catalog Card Number 99-074797
Copyright © September 1999

Art Direction and Layout
Kimberly N. Bender

Editing and Proofing
Bryan R. Beaver

Printed by
DATA REPRODUCTIONS
Auburn Hills, Michigan

REEDSWAIN INC
612 Pughtown Road
Spring City, PA 19081
1-800-331-5191
www.reedswain.com

120
Competitive Games
and
Training Exercises

NICOLA PICA

published by
REEDSWAIN INC

INTRODUCTION

In match-like games competition and team spirit are enhanced, they help to stimulate attention and concentration and call for precision and ball control. Match-like games are fundamental to coaching. However, they cannot be used on their own or in isolation but must be integrated with other coaching activities. Such games should focus on time, space, speed and rhythm as well as dexterity, coordination, strength, flexibility, and balance.

The coach should use these small sided games to develop his players' skills and tactical awareness, adjusting them, where necessary, according to their technical ability.

"...you can discover more about one person
in one hour of play than in a
year of conversation"

Plato

GAME 1

OBJECTIVE

- Controlling the ball with the head.
- Dribbling and space orientation.
- Aerobic muscular conditioning.

Individual game.

Playing area: different areas can be used: the midfield circle, the penalty area or an area marked with cones, the size depending on the number of players. The area should not be too large to force the players to play in restricted spaces.

Some balls are placed every 3-4 yards outside the playing area. One player is outside while the others are inside.

The outside player tries to hit the inside players with a header.

The header can be made:

1. while walking or running slowly: around the outside of the playing area, throw the ball up with the hands and then head it;
2. starting with the ball in the hands, kick it upward with the instep of the foot and then head it;
3. starting with the ball in the hands, let it bounce, kick it up and head it;
4. while walking, kick the ball up with the instep of the foot and let the ball bounce, kick it up and head it.

The player should practice these different ways to head the ball, in a varied sequence.

Each player inside the playing area dribbles a ball in the direction shown by the coach, avoiding being hit by the ball headed by the outside player.

The player who hits the highest number of inside players is the winner.

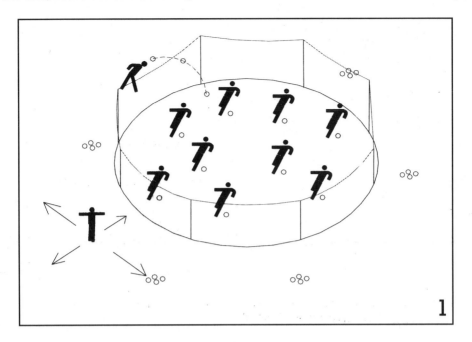

1

COACHING POINTS

When heading, the ball must be hit with the forehead; take-off using one foot only and the last step must be longer.

When kicking the ball: the instep of the foot must be outstretched and the leg follows the ball.

When dribbling on the right, the ball must be touched with the outside of the right foot (the area of the little toe) and with the inside of the left foot (the area around the base of the big toe); vice versa when dribbling it on the left.

GAME 2

OBJECTIVE

- Controlling the ball with the head.
- Dribbling and space orientation.
- Aerobic muscular conditioning.

Team game.

This game is played by two teams, white and black, placed opposite each other at the ends of the playing area.

Playing area: different size areas can be used: the midfield circle, the penalty area or a cone-marked area the dimensions depending on the number of players, but which should not be too large.

Balls are placed around the outside.

Every player has a ball.

One player, in white, is placed outside the playing area: like in GAME 1 he tries to hit the players in black with a header.

The players in black dribble the ball using only one foot in the direction shown by the coach. The team in white tries to disrupt their movement by moving without restrictions while juggling using a combination of bounces and touches with the instep and the thigh.

After two minutes the teams exchange roles.

The team that hits the highest number of opponents is the winner.

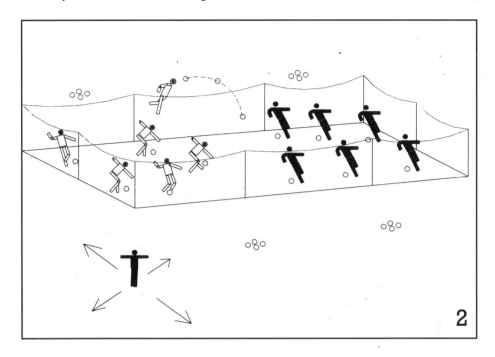

COACHING POINTS

When heading, the ball must be hit with the forehead; take-off using one foot only and the last step must be longer.
When kicking the ball: the instep of the foot must be outstretched and the leg follows the ball.
   When dribbling on the right, the ball must be touched with the outside of the right foot (the area of the little toe) and with the inside of the left foot (the area around the base of the big toe); vice versa when dribbling it on the left.

GAME 3

OBJECTIVE

- Development of the players' vision and awareness.
- Development of pressing and forcing in defense.
- Improvement of aerobic conditioning.

Team game.
This game is played by two teams.
Playing area: different size areas can be used: the midfield circle, the penalty area or a cone-marked area the dimensions depending on the number of players, but which should not be too large.

Balls are placed around the outside.

One player in white is placed outside the playing area: like in GAME 1 he tries to hit the players in black by heading.

Both teams inside the playing area must be equal in numbers.

The players in black each have a ball and dribble without restrictions. The players in white tackle them shoulder to shoulder, trying to force them outside. The roles are reversed after five minutes.

The team that hits the highest number of opponents is the winner.

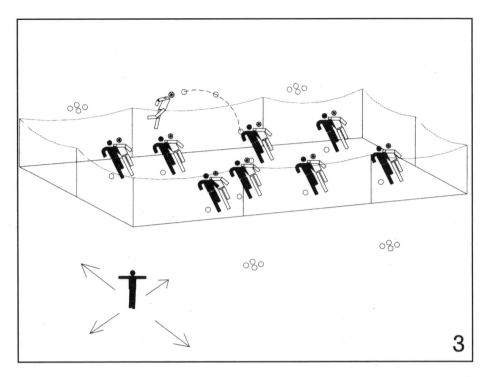

COACHING POINTS

Dribble the ball using the foot on the opposite side from the approaching defender.

The defender can only use his shoulders, not his arms or hands.

The shoulder tackle should be made when the player with the ball has his weight on the foot furthest away from the defender, timing his tackle to easily push his opponent off balance.

GAME 4

OBJECTIVE

- Development of the players' vision and awareness.
- Controlling the ball in the air while moving.
- Improvement of aerobic conditioning and reactions.

Team game: played by 2 teams.

Playing area: an area marked by two parallel lines of cones, starting from the midfield line up to the top of the penalty area. The width between the two lines of cones can be adjusted according to the number of players: it should not be too wide in order to stimulate close ball control.

Each player has a ball.

The white team tries to score from the penalty area: its players move forward from the midfield, juggling with all the parts of the body trying to reach the penalty area and shoot at goal.

The players can let it bounce once or more times, kick it up and forward with the instep, then sprint to reach it and juggle it again.

The players in black face the team in white without contact, each of them has a ball and their task is to throw it to hit the opponent's ball only when it touches the ground.

The roles are reversed after five minutes.

The team that scores more goals is the winner

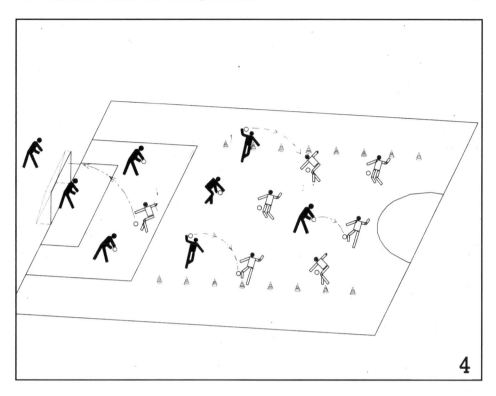

4

COACHING POINTS

When juggling, the instep is outstretched and so is the leg, which follows the ball. The ball should go up without spinning.

In sideways movements it is better to juggle the ball with the foot farther from the direction where one wishes to go, with the right foot in a sideways movement to the left. In this way the ball can be played better for a pass, a shot or for dribbling past an opponent.

The defender, when facing an opponent, should keep his legs slightly apart and move to the side of the supporting foot of the juggling player.

GAME 5

OBJECTIVE

- Dribbling at speed.
- Improving reaction times and acceleration.
- Developing endurance and speed and speed with the ball.
- High shots, lobs.

Team game: played by 2 teams.

Playing area: an area marked by two parallel lines of cones, starting from the midfield line up to the top of the penalty area. The width between the two lines of cones can be adjusted according to the number of players: it should not be very wide in order to stimulate close ball control. Place a line of flags just outside the six yard area.

The team in black starts at the center of the field and each player has a ball. The team in white is divided into two groups behind the goal line, on either side of the goal, sitting with their backs to the field.

White players A, B and C have a ball, they are sitting with their backs to the field at the half way line.

When the coach gives the signal, the players in black dribble as quickly as possible in a straight line using long strides and touching the ball every 7-8 yards.

Players A, B and C quickly get up and sprint back to tackle the attackers.

When the fastest of the players in black get near the penalty area the coach gives a second signal.

From the sides of the goal, the players in white sprint to the front of the flags to challenge the attackers.

The players in black change their speed, bringing the ball under close control and, before the players in white can tackle them, they lob at goal. If a player in white wins the ball he clears it out or to the center of the field.

The opponents who lose the ball stop playing and go outside the field, where they wait for the next phase of the game.

Each goal scores two points.

The teams defend and attack alternately.

The team that scores more points is the winner.

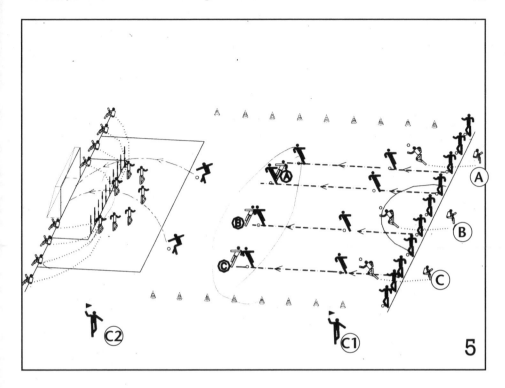

COACHING POINTS

The ball must be dribbled forward in a straight line.

Dribble using the lower part of the instep.

When shooting kick under the ball and keep the supporting foot behind it.

GAME 6

OBJECTIVE

- Dribbling at speed.
- Change of speed.
- Coaching muscular awareness.
- Improving reaction times and acceleration.
- Low-ground shots.

Team game: played by 2 teams.

Playing area: half field.
Place some flags in the front of the six yard area. Place two parallel lines of cones from the midfield to the penalty area (see diagram).

Each player has a number and a ball.

The teams are arranged inside the midfield circle, one on the right and the other on the left.

The teams carry out juggling exercises.

When the coach calls out a number the player dribbles, zigzagging through the cones at speed.

When they reach the penalty area they shoot at goal without hitting the flags.

The player who reaches the penalty area first scores a point. Each goal scores a point too, therefore if a player is the first to reach the penalty area and also scores a goal he will get two points. The team with the higher score at the end of five minutes is the winner.

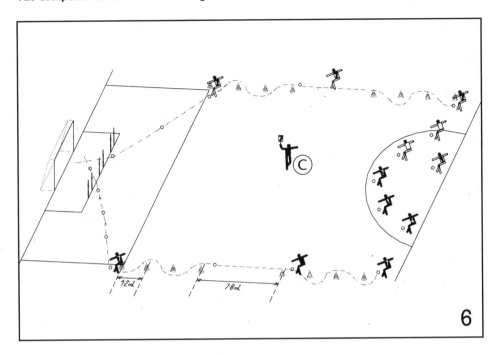

COACHING POINTS

Dribble the ball forward in a straight line; touch it in the lower part with the outstretched instep.

Run with long steps so as to increase speed.

While zigzagging through the cones keep the ball under the upper body.

When shooting, the tip of the supporting foot should point in the direction one wishes to send the ball and be kept slightly forward and near the ball. When kicking, pivot on the supporting leg and slightly rotate the upper body in the direction one wishes to send the ball.

GAME 7

OBJECTIVE

- Awareness.
- Coaching speed.
- Coaching direct and accurate passes.
- Endurance/speed.

Team game: played by 2 teams.

Playing area: half field.

A parallel line of cones for each player is placed at a distance of 6-7 yards from the midfield line. The players with the same number make up a pair. Each pair of players is placed in front of two lines of cones and carries out an exercise in twos with two balls. The two players start diagonally to each other at a distance of about 10 yards: they pass the ball to each other perpendicularly and run square to get the pass. Every 20-25 seconds, the coach (who has two balls in his hands) calls out a number, these players sprint dribbling through the cones of the line opposite them. The coach throws up the two balls and the players leave their ball and sprint to one of the two balls thrown up by the coach and shoot at goal.

Then, they retrieve the ball they have kicked and return to the starting position.

The player who gets to the ball first scores a point.

Each goal scored equals one point, so the player who is first on the ball and scores gets two points.

The team which scores more points is the winner.

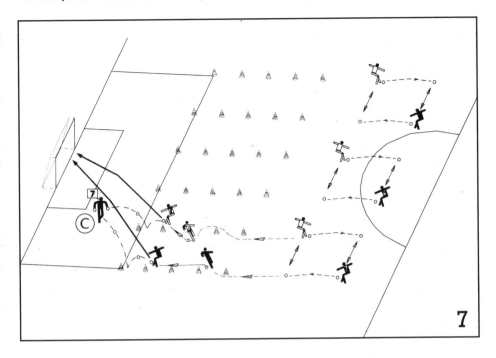

COACHING POINTS

Accuracy of passing and dribbling under control.

GAME 8

OBJECTIVE

- Awareness
- Speed.
- Coaching direct and accurate passes.
- Endurance/speed.

This is a variation of game 7.
The coach throws up only one ball and the players leave their ball and sprint to this ball. The player who is first shoots at goal, while the other tries to tackle him. Each goal scores one point.

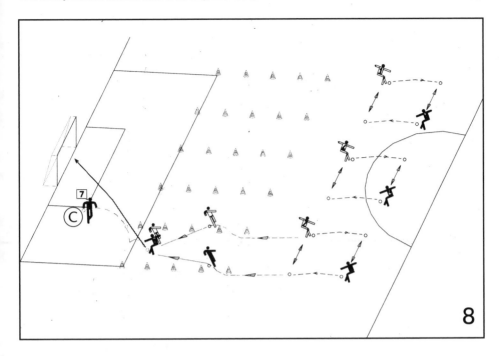

COACHING POINTS

Accurate passing, dribbling at speed, shooting first time

GAME 9

OBJECTIVE

- Awareness.
- Coaching speed.
- Coaching direct passes.
- Endurance/Speed.
- Accurate passing.

Team game: played by 2 teams.
Playing area: half field.
One team attacks and the other defends. Two five-yard lines are formed, each made up of 5 cones. The distance between the two lines should be about 8 yards. In between the two lines, two flags are placed at a distance of 5 yards from one another. The teams are placed opposite each other, at a distance of 5 yards from the flags.

    The first player in white passes the ball through the flags to the player in black who is first in the line; he then sprints and zigzags through the cones on his right, then goes to the back of his line. The first player in black passes the ball back through the flags to the next player in white, sprints and zigzags through the cones on his right and then goes to the back of his line. The exercise continues with the other players.

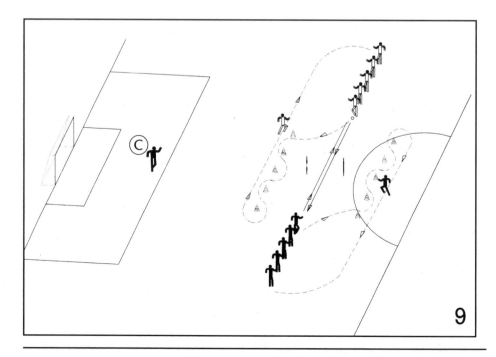

9

The coach is inside the penalty area: when he gives a signal and throws up the ball, the first player of each line sprints to win possession. The player in black tries to score, while the one in white tries to pass it to his teammate who, in order to receive the pass, quickly moves to him from the back of the line immediately when he sees that his teammate has won the ball and they play a 1-2 back to the end of the line. The other players in the midfield should keep on doing the exercise.

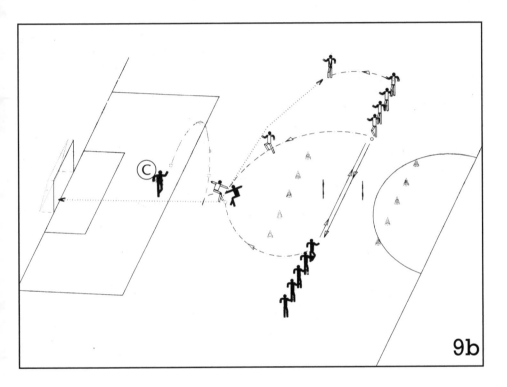

COACHING POINTS

Each goal scores 2 points.
Each accurate pass to the teammate scores 2 points.

GAME 10

OBJECTIVE

- Ability to make long throw-ins.
- Recovering and sprinting.
- Low passes to an on-coming teammate.
- Improving passing accuracy.
- Development of endurance and speed.

Team game: played by 2 teams.
Playing area: half field.
Two parallel lines of cones should be placed from the penalty area to the halfway line.

The two teams mix and form two lines, A and B, made up of alternate players in white and black. The players are sitting in two lines opposite each other, at a distance of 15 yards. From the sitting position, the first player (in black) of line A "Throws-In" the ball diagonally forward to the right, then immediately gets up and moves diagonally forward to his left. At the same time, the first player (in white) of line B gets up quickly, sprints to the ball "Thrown-In" by the first player of line A and makes a direct volley-pass to the running player in black who, in turn, makes a direct first time pass to the first player sitting in line B (in black).

This player "Throws-In" the ball and the next player in white from line A makes a direct volley-pass to the running teammate.

Each player sits down at the end of the opposite line after making the pass.

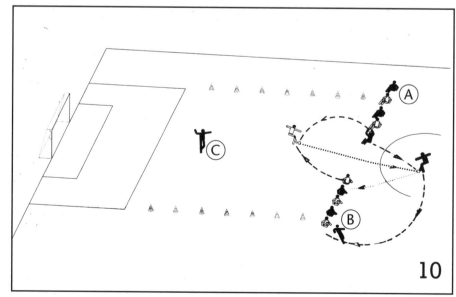

10

The coach gives a signal and throws the ball into the cone-marked area at a moment when the two players of the respective groups kick the ball. These two players and the two at the back of their respective lines (one in black and one in white) immediately sprint to the ball thrown by the coach and play a 2 v 2 and shoot at goal in the cone-marked area and in the penalty area. A goal is valid only if at least one pass has been made. Meanwhile the group exercise in the midfield continues.

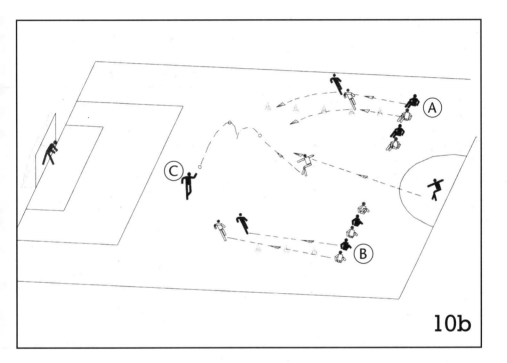

COACHING POINTS

Accurate passing and first time passing and shooting.

GAME 11

OBJECTIVE

- Passing with quick changes of position.
- Receiving the ball with the inside of the foot.
- Speed and endurance.
- Shooting at goal and shooting with the inside of the instep of the foot.
- Crossing to the running teammate.
- Good timing for sprinting and crossing.

Team game: played by 2 teams.
Playing area: half field.
The players in midfield carry out an exercise in groups of three: each group has a number and is made up of two players in black (A and B) playing as forwards, and one in white (C) playing as a defender. They play in a cone-marked 10 yard square, and each in one corner: B passes the ball to C and runs to the free corner. C goes to the ball and controls it with the inside of the right foot; then he passes it to A and runs to the free corner (where B was before). A goes to the ball, controls it with the inside of the right foot, and passes it to B and runs to the free corner etc. The exercise goes on like this until the coach kicks a ball onto the wing and calls out a number of a group. The three players of the group called quickly run to the ball. If the two in black are the first on the ball they zigzag pass the ball to each other, with the player in white actively defending them.

When they are near the penalty area, the outside player in black crosses the ball to his teammate, who has moved into the penalty area to shoot. When the first group has shot the three players return to their square and continue the exercise, reversing the direction of the passes. The coach passes a ball to the other wing and calls another number.

Each goal scores a point for the players in black. If the player in white is able to win the ball and pass it accurately to the coach he scores two points.

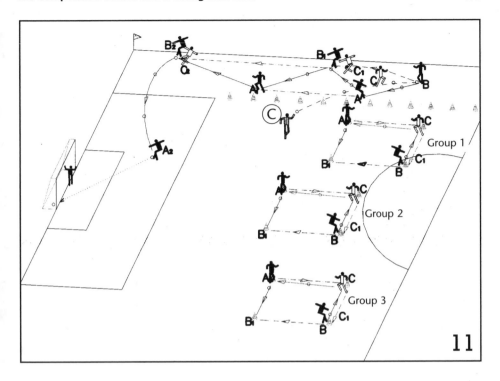

11

COACHING POINTS

Passes with the inside of the foot.

Crosses with the inside of the instep.

Receiving the ball with the inside of the foot: take up a 45-degree position to the coming ball just a moment before it reaches the foot. The supporting foot hops slightly, in order to turn the body to the direction where one wants to play the ball. When the ball arrives, raise the foot about 2 inches from the ground while moving it backwards to absorb the shock: push the ball firmly in the desired direction.

GAME 12

OBJECTIVE

- Developing the instep feel for the ball in a straight and 45-degree space.
- Dexterity with speed and endurance..
- Crosses to the near post, to the far post and to the center of the penalty area.
- Speed off the ball.
- Volley clearance.

Team game: played by 2 teams.
Playing area: form a corridor from the penalty area to the midfield line. Place one player outside the corridor with a disrupting task.

Form a circuit in midfield. Each player has a number and the players with the same number form a pair.

Place 3 cones to form a 6 yard triangle. The player in black throws the ball to the cone in front of him. His partner in white, starting from the left, runs to the ball and after it has bounced volleys it back to the player in black with the instep. He then runs quickly around the cone on his right and back to the center to volley the next ball after it has bounced. And so on, continuing to sprint and turn and volley for one minute before changing roles.

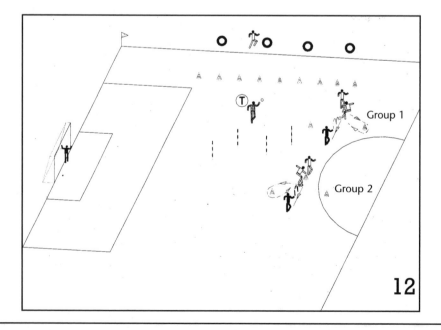

Group 1

Group 2

12

The coach kicks a ball to the wing and calls out a number of a pair. The player in black sprints to the ball, dribbles it down the wing to the penalty area and then crosses.

The player in white sprints to the penalty area to clear the cross made by his opponent.

While the player in black dribbles the ball, the player in white outside the field becomes a passive defender.

Each cross cleared scores one point for the defending team, while failure to clear the ball scores a point for the attacking team.

After 5 minutes the roles are reversed.

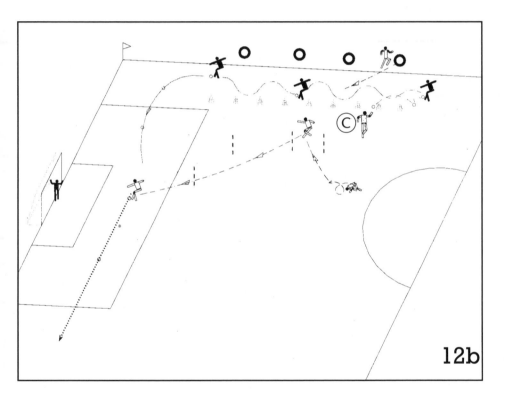

12b

COACHING POINTS

Pass with the instep: the tip of the foot is outstretched and the leg follows the ball.

GAME 13

OBJECTIVE

- Speed of movement on the wings.
- Alternating aerobic endurance and speed endurance.
- Getting used to the idea that the ball is not "mine" but "the team's".

Team game: played by 2 teams.
Playing area: half field with one goal at each end. Form a side corridor with cones on both wings.

Place one player from each team on each wing with the task to make crosses. Each of them has a handkerchief hanging from his waist.

The teams play a regular match, but a goal can only be scored after a cross from the players on the wings, who do not challenge each other.

An opponent can enter the wing only when the winger has possession of the ball, chasing him in order to pull his handkerchief off.

If the opponent succeeds in pulling it off he can then throw the ball in.

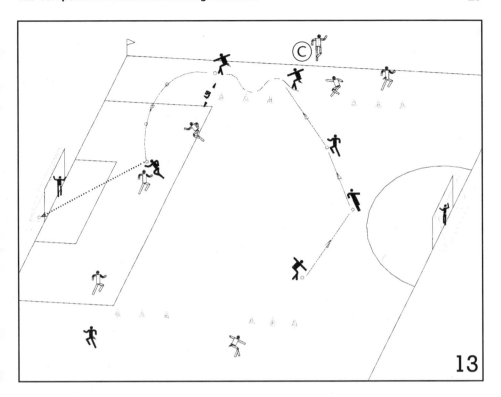

13

COACHING POINTS

Get used to looking where the ball can be crossed before receiving it.

The winger should move at speed with the ball and cross before being tagged.

Cross to the near post, to the far one or to center of the penalty area.

GAME 14

> ## OBJECTIVE
>
> • Speed of movement on the wings.
> • Alternating aerobic endurance and speed endurance.
> • Getting used to the idea that the ball is not "mine" but "the team's".

Team game: it is a variation of game 13.

The players in black play as attackers, those in white as defenders.

The team in black places one player on both wings with the task to make crosses. They both have a handkerchief hanging from their waist.

A goal can only be scored after a cross from one of the wingers.

The defenders clear the ball to the midfield and can enter the wing only when the winger has possession of the ball. If they succeed in pulling the handkerchief off from the winger they can throw the ball in and clear it to the midfield.

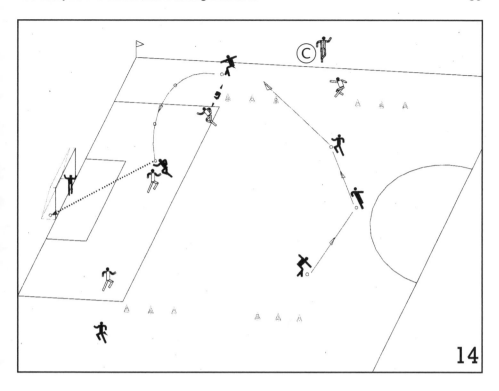

COACHING POINTS

Get used to looking where the ball can be crossed before receiving it.
 The winger should move at speed with the ball and cross early.
 Cross to the near post, to the far post or to the center of the penalty area.

GAME 15

OBJECTIVE

- One-two passes.
- Criss-crossing.
- Deep passes.
- Shots at goal.
- Speed of movement.
- Alternating aerobic/endurance/speed activity.
- Well timed sprinting at irregular intervals.

Team game: it is a variation of game 14.

Playing area: half field with one goal. Form a central corridor with cones.

The players in black are the attackers, those in white the defenders.

The team in black places one player with a handkerchief hanging from his waist in the central corridor. His task is to find ways to attack and his teammates search for passes from him as they criss-cross and carry out deep penetrating runs to receive his long passes. He can also make square passes.

A goal can only be scored with a header or a volley after a pass from the player in the corridor.

The players in white clear the ball to the midfield and can enter the corridor when the central opponent has possession of the ball. If they succeed in pulling the handkerchief off they can throw the ball in and clear it to the midfield.

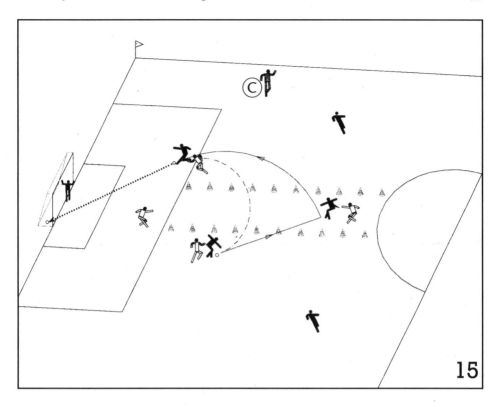

COACHING POINTS

The ball is not "mine", it's the "team's".

The number of passes before shooting at goal can be adjusted according to the players' skills.

GAME 16

OBJECTIVE

- Speed and endurance.
- Thinking even when not in possession of the ball.
- Developing the instep feel for the ball.
- Drop kicks.
- Speed of movement.
- Alternating aerobic work.
- Headers.

Team game: played by 2 teams.
Playing area: half field, one goal at each end. Each player has a handkerchief hanging from his waist.

Starting with the ball in their hands, the players make passes with the instep, by drop kick and with a header.

If one player succeeds in pulling the handkerchief off the opponent who has the ball in his hands then he throws the ball in, or he drop-kicks it or kicks it with the instep from the point where he pulled off the handkerchief.

A goal can be scored with a header.

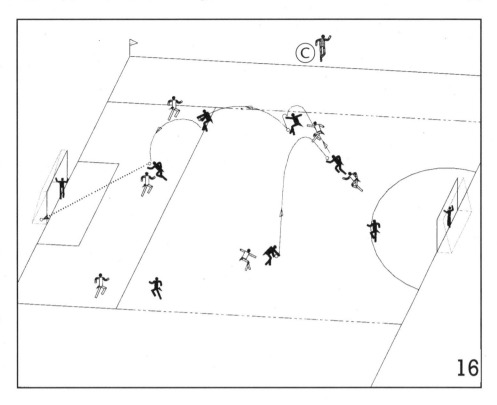

COACHING POINTS

Get used to looking where the ball can be passed before receiving it.

GAME 17

OBJECTIVE

• Speed of movement.

Team game: played by 2 teams.
Playing area: half field, with one goal at each end.
Each player has a handkerchief hanging from his waist.
The two teams play a regular match on the half field.
The ball is won when the player of one team succeeds in pulling off the handkerchief from the opponent in possession of the ball.

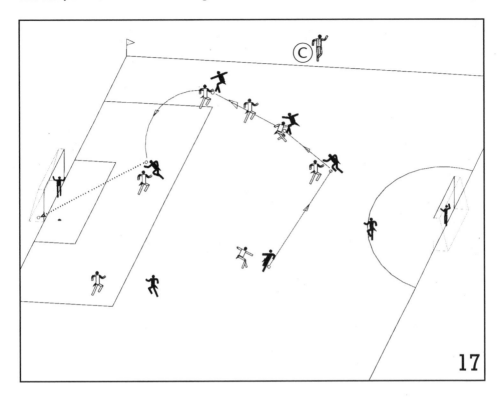

COACHING POINTS

Get used to looking where the ball can be passed before receiving it.

GAME 18

OBJECTIVE

- Speed off the ball.
- Speed with the ball.

Team game: played by 2 teams.

Playing area: an area marked with two parallel lines of cones from the penalty area to the half way line.

The players in black have the ball, those in white split into two groups (A and B): the players of group A run after the opponents, those of group B have an interfering task.

Each player in black has a handkerchief hanging from his waist and has possession of a ball.

The players in black are arranged along the midfield line and those of group A are sitting behind them at a distance of 10 yards.

The players of group B each have a ball and are arranged along the edge of the penalty area.

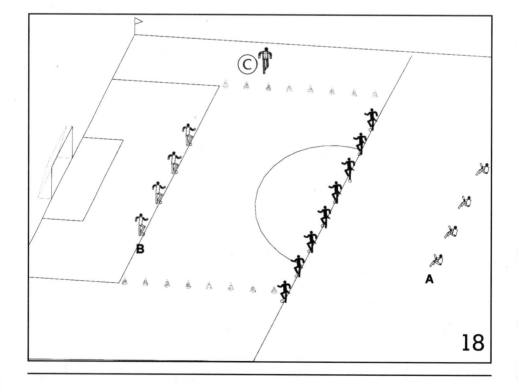

When the coach whistles, the players in black dribble the ball forward at speed to the penalty area, without leaving the cone-marked area.

The players of group A get up quickly and sprint after the opponents in black to pull the handkerchief from their waist.

The players of group B move forward to delay the attackers.

Each handkerchief pulled off before reaching the penalty area scores one point.

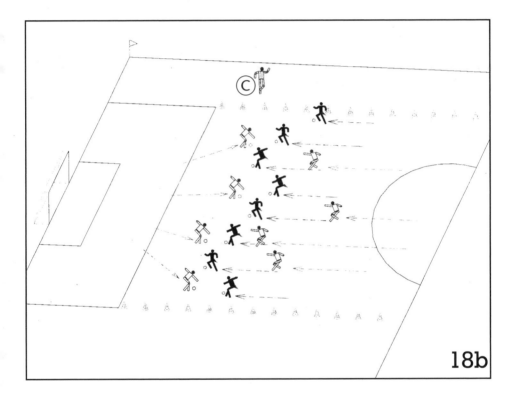

18b

COACHING POINTS

Dribbling at speed, under control.

GAME 19

OBJECTIVE

- Speed off the ball.
- Speed and endurance.
- Dribbling at speed.
- One-two passes.
- Shooting with the instep.

Team game: played by 2 teams.

Playing area: half field, with only one goal. A line of flags is placed just outside the penalty area. Each player in both teams has his own number; the players in black have a handkerchief hanging from their waists.

The players in black are in pairs 8 yards apart: A starts with the ball in his hands and passes it with the instep to B who is in a sitting position. B immediately gets up, controls the ball as he prefers and lets it bounce, then he passes it back to A and sits down again, and so on.

Reverse roles every 3 minutes.

At the same time the players in white are at 10 yards from their opponents, with their backs to the goal juggling a ball using alternate feet.

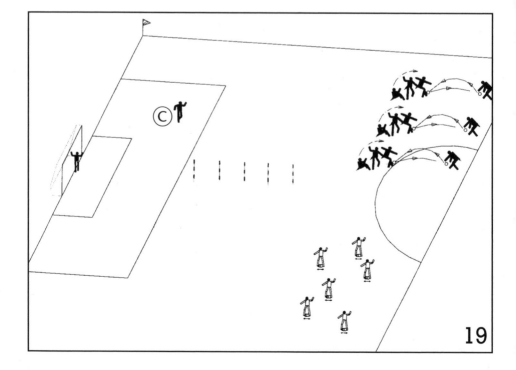

19

The coach calls out a number, that black player immediately dribbles the ball at speed through the flags, then he makes a one-two pass with the coach and shoots at goal.

At the same time the corresponding player in white leaves his ball and runs after the player in black, trying to pull off his handkerchief before he can make the one-two pass with the coach.

Each goal scores two points, while each pulled-off handkerchief scores one.

After six minutes the roles are reversed.

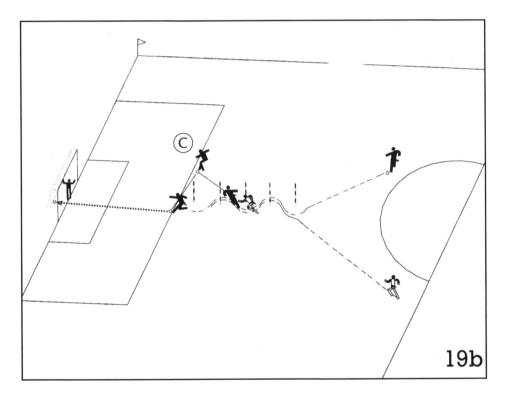

19b

COACHING POINTS
Shots at goal:
- the tip of the supporting foot is turned in the direction one wants to shoot the ball;
- the supporting foot is slightly forward and near the ball (in this way the ball, which is moving, reaches the same line as the supporting foot by the time the ball is kicked);
- the kicking leg follows the ball;

GAME 20

OBJECTIVE

- Speed off the ball.
- Speed with the ball.
- Dribbling.
- Awareness.

Team game: played by 2 teams.
Playing area: half field, with cones, hoops and hurdles scattered. Each player in black has a handkerchief hanging from his waist and has a ball.

The team in black is in a line parallel to the halfway line, while the players in white are in a prone position along the midfield line 10 yards from the opponents.

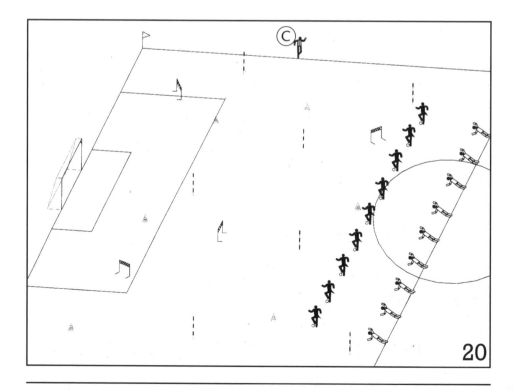

20

When the coach gives the signal, the players in black dribble the ball forward at speed through the obstacles to the penalty area. At the same time the players in white get up and run after the opponents trying to pull the handkerchiefs off.

Each handkerchief that is pulled off before reaching the penalty area scores one point.

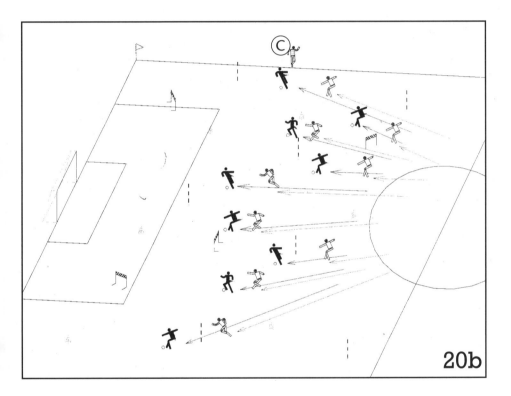

COACHING POINTS

Dribbling at speed and changing direction.

GAME 21

OBJECTIVE

- Speed with the ball.
- Dribbling.
- Awareness.

Team game: it is a variation of game 20.
The players in black have a handkerchief hanging from their waists and start in a line parallel to the halfway line with a ball each.
   The players in white start 5 yards behind their opponents with a ball.

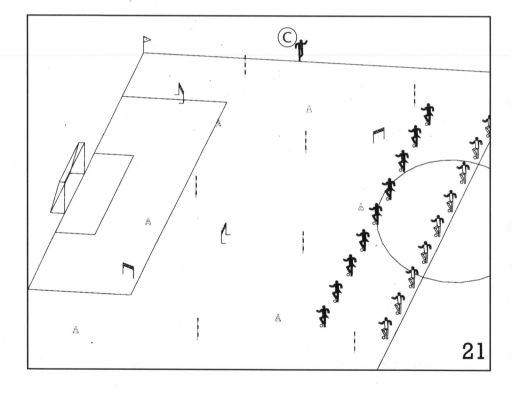

When the coach gives the signal, the players in black dribble the ball through the obstacles to the penalty area. At the same time the players in white start dribbling forward too, trying to pull off the opponents' hand-kerchiefs before they enter the penalty area.

Each handkerchief pulled off scores one point.

After each repetition the roles are reversed.

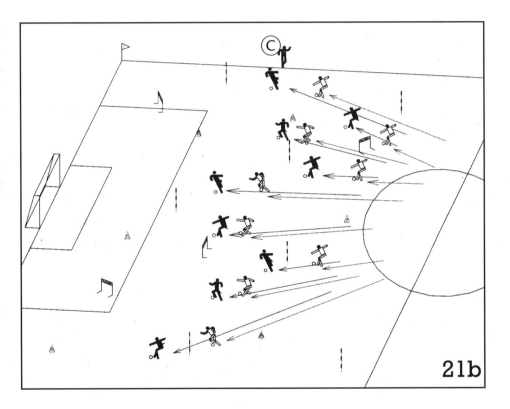

COACHING POINTS

Dribbling at speed and changing direction

GAME 22

OBJECTIVE

- Speed off the ball.
- Speed with the ball.
- Dribbling.
- Awareness.

Team game: it is a variation of game 21.
The players of both teams control and dribble two balls at the same time.

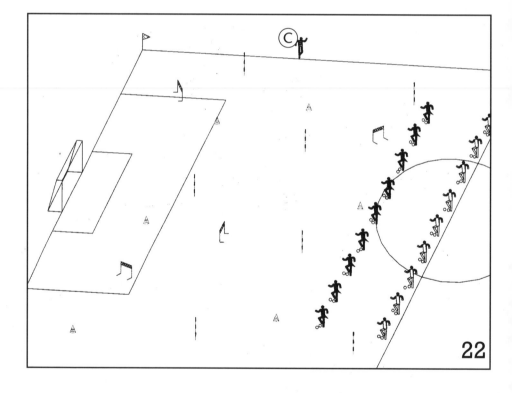

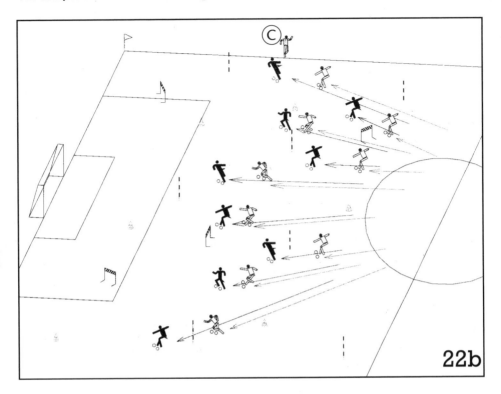

COACHING POINTS

Do not sacrifice control for speed

GAME 23

OBJECTIVE

- Speed off the ball.
- Speed of movement.
- Playing with superiority and inferiority in numbers.
- Shots at goal.
- Awareness.
- One-two passes.

Team game: played by 2 teams on a full field.

The players in black, each with a handkerchief hanging from his waist, carry out an attack; the players in white split into two groups, A and B. The players of group A are the defenders while group B are on the edge of the other penalty area and recover and chase back.

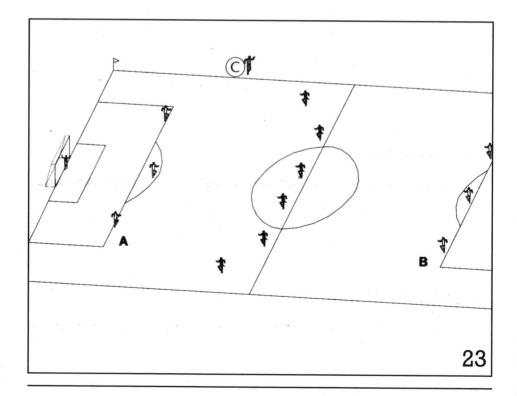

23

When the coach whistles, the players in black move forward and try to score a goal, challenged by the players of group A who clear the ball to the midfield if they win it.

At the same time the players of group B start from the edge of the other penalty area and run after the players in black, trying to pull off their handkerchiefs.

The player whose handkerchief is pulled off goes out of the field: therefore the attackers must try to score before group B manages to pull off the handkerchiefs from all of them.

A repetition finishes after all the attackers have been sent out of the field or after a shot at goal.

After each repetition the roles are reversed.

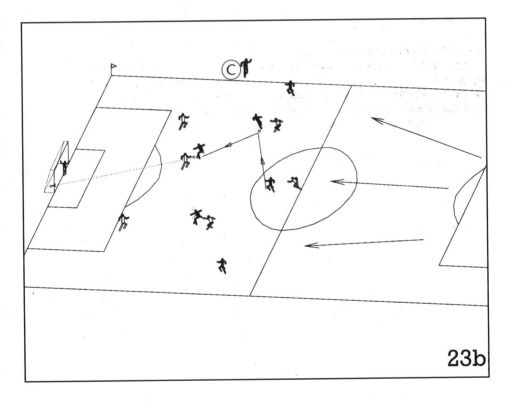

23b

COACHING POINTS

Movement off the ball and quick passing.

GAME 24

OBJECTIVE

- Speed off the ball.
- Playing with superiority and inferiority in numbers.
- Shots at goal.
- Awareness.
- One-two passes.

Team game: played by 2 teams on a full field.
The players in black attack; those in white split into two groups, A and B.
Group A starts at the top of the penalty area and defends the goal, group
B starts at the other penalty area: they must win a speed competition with
the players in black. A circuit is formed between the halfway line and the
penalty area in group B's half of the field.

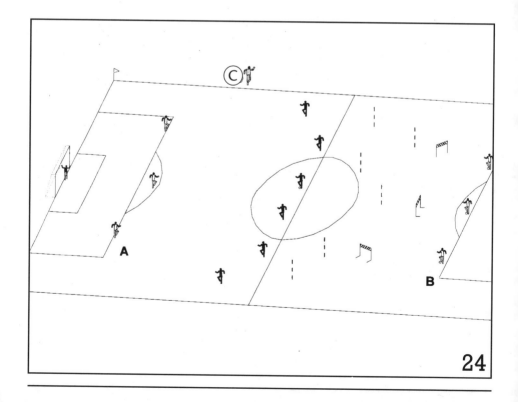

24

When the coach whistles, the players in black start attack the goal from the halfway line. If defenders A intercept the ball they clear it to midfield. Meanwhile, the players of group B dribble through the circuit and back to the starting point at speed.

The players in black must try to score before all the players of group B have returned to the starting point.

After each repetition the roles are reversed.

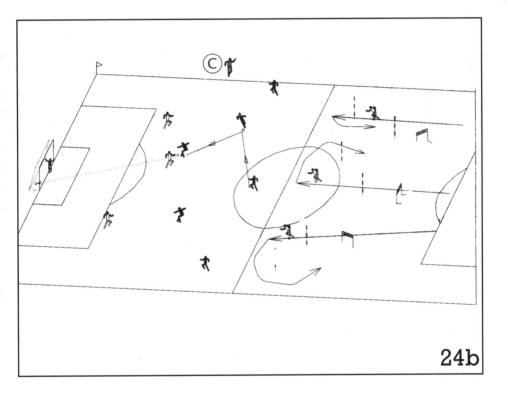

24b

COACHING POINTS

Attack at speed with quick 1-2 passing moves, dribbling under control at speed.

GAME 25

OBJECTIVE

- Speed off the ball.
- Juggling the ball in a small space.
- Diving headers.
- Shots at goal.
- Zigzag running with feints (the player is stimulated to run and feint to the right and the left to keep his opponents from pulling off his handkerchief).

Team game: played by 2 teams.
Playing area: half field; the goal is divided into three parts by using two flags: the central part is wider and is given a lower score than the other two.

The coach is in the penalty area with the ball.

The players in white are in the prone position, arms bent and hands under their shoulders. Two goalkeepers are opposite them and throw them the ball with a low trajectory: the players quickly get up and dive forward, heading the ball back to the goalkeeper.

The players in black have a handkerchief hanging from their waists: they are inside a 5 yard square, 10 yards in front of the white team. Each player juggles in the following sequence: let the ball bounce once, kick it with the instep, head it and then let it bounce on the ground again.

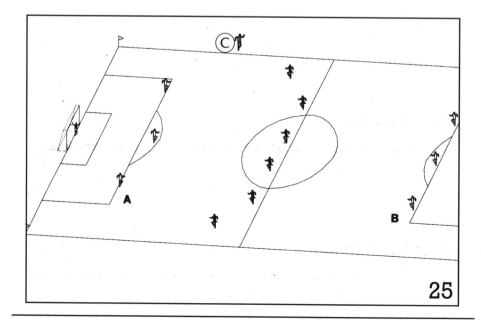

25

At this moment the coach kicks the ball and calls out a number. The respective players in white and black sprint forward, the player in black runs to the ball to shoot at goal, while the player in white runs after him in order to pull off his handkerchief before he shoots at goal. The player whose handkerchief is pulled off cannot shoot.

Each shot scores the points corresponding to the goal section it goes through. After 5 minutes the roles are reversed.

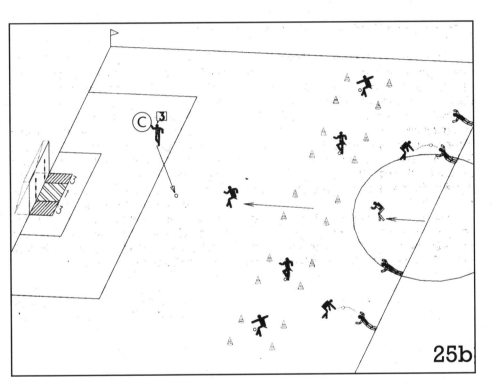

25b

COACHING POINTS

Headers:
- head the ball with the center of the forehead.

Juggling:
- the instep must be outstretched;
- the leg follows the ball;
- receive the ball with the center of the forehead with the body under the ball;

GAME 26

OBJECTIVE

- Speed off the ball.
- Speed with the ball.
- Dribbling.
- Receiving the ball and turning.

Team game: played by 2 teams.

Playing area: the midfield circle.

Place one line of balls and one of cones inside the midfield line, at a distance of 8-9 yards from each other; the distance between the cones and balls should be 2 yards.

The players of each team have corresponding numbers and practice 180-degree turns.

The teams are divided in groups of three and are arranged outside the midfield circle. The group in white is on the side of the balls while the one in black is on the side of the cones: the players with the same number must have the same ranking in the line.

Players A-B-C of each group form a line and are placed at a distance of 15 yards from each other. A passes to B who goes to the ball, pivots on his left foot and with the inside of the right foot turns to the right to C; then B passes to C, who controls the ball and passes it back to B who, pivoting on the right foot, with the inside of his left foot turns and passes to A, and so forth.

During this exercise the coach passes the ball and calls out a number, 7. Player 7 in black sprints to the ball, controls it, turns backward to his right and dribbles the ball through the cones.

At the same time player 7 in white runs to the line of balls and slaloms through them putting his right foot in the spaces between the balls, thus making a sort of spinning movement to the right. After he has reached the end of the ball line he goes back to the starting point by slaloming through the balls, this time putting his left foot in the spaces between the balls, thus making a sort of spinning movement to the left.

The player who is the first to get out of the midfield circle scores a point for his team.

When the players reach their group they switch places.

After a certain number of goes the roles are reversed.

The winner is the team that has scored more points after an established number of goes.

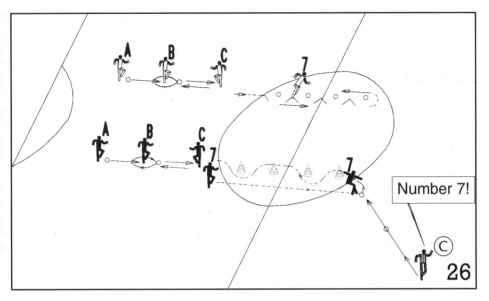

COACHING POINTS

The player can turn to the right with the ball in three ways:

- The player goes to the ball and puts forward the inside of the receiving right foot, which he pulls back as soon as he touches the ball. At the same time, he pivots on the supporting left foot and makes a 45-degree angle. The ball rolls on and the weight of the body shifts on the right leg. The left foot moves and gives the next touch to the ball.

- With the inside of the left foot the player touches the rolling ball slightly so as to make it pass behind the supporting right leg, which is ahead of the ball. The player pivots on the right foot and turns. The left foot follows the ball, keeping it under control.

- The player goes to the ball and makes a quick movement to the left with the right foot, as if wishing to make a pass or turn to the left with the inside of the right foot. He lets the ball roll and the touches it with the outside of the right foot, shifting the ball slowly to the right: at the same time he shifts the weight of the body on the right leg. He turns by pivoting on the right foot and dribbles the ball forward with the left.

DRIBBLING ALONG THE CIRCLE

- Dribble the ball with the outside of the right foot, clockwise.
- Dribble the ball with the outside of the left foot, counterclockwise.
- Dribble the ball with the inside of the right foot, counterclockwise.
- Dribble the ball with the inside of the left foot, clockwise.

GAME 27

OBJECTIVE

- Ability to turn.
- Passing and exchanging positions.
- Improvement of endurance.

Relay game: played by two teams.
Each team is divided into two groups.

The groups of each team form lines as shown in the diagram: the distance between the players of a group is 8-10 yards, while the distance between the groups is 20-25 yards.

One player, O, is placed between the two lines of his teammates.

When the coach gives the signal, player L makes a direct pass to O; O goes to the ball, controls, turns and then passes to A; then he sprints and exchange positions with player A.

In the meanwhile player L sprints quickly to the center in order to get the ball from A and pass it to player I. The game goes on like this, turning, passing and exchanging positions with the teammate whom the pass has been made to, until all the players of the team have had their go.

The team that is first at finishing a go scores a point.

The winner is the team who reaches the established score first.

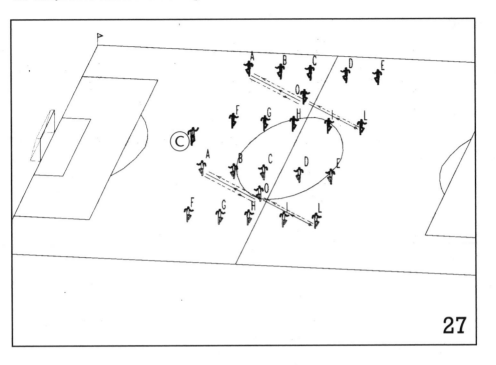

COACHING POINTS

How to turn: see GAME 26.

Two players can be placed in the center, between the two groups of each team, if the players are slow in exchanging their positions.

GAME 28

OBJECTIVE

- Turning and passing.
- Passing and sprinting forward.
- Speed with the ball.
- Speed off the ball.
- Development of the ability to use strength according to distance in passes.

Relay game.

The exercise is based on turning and immediately passing the ball.

One team forms a line behind square A, marked with cones 2-3 yards apart.

About 12-15 yards from A, another cone-marked 2-3 yard square is formed (B).

One player, O, is placed opposite his teammates, at a distance of 7-8 yards. He must turn and pass the ball. When the coach gives the signal the first player of the line passes the ball to his teammate O and quickly runs to square B. Player O goes to the ball, turns and passes it to square B with the inside of the foot, where the first player of the line now can get the ball, turn with it around a cone, pass it back to O and then go outside square B, so as to form a new line. Player O goes to the ball, turns and passes it to the second player of the line who repeats the same movements as the first player.

The exercise goes on like this until all the players are behind square B, forming a new line.

At this point player O goes to the back of the line and the first player takes his place. The exercise continues until all the players in turn have played the role of O.

The team that finishes the exercise first scores a point.

The winner is the team that reaches the established score first.

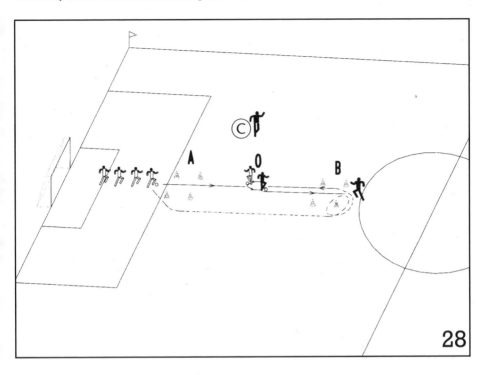

COACHING POINTS

How to turn:
- as for player O, see GAME 26.
- dribbling around the cone:
    - with the outside of the right foot, turn to the right and pass with the left foot;
    - with the outside of the left foot, turn to the left and pass with the right foot;
    - with the inside of the left foot, turn to the right and pass with the left foot;
    - with the inside of the right foot, turn to the left and pass with the right foot.

GAME 29

OBJECTIVE

- Ability to turn and pass.
- Turn and dribble the ball along a circle.
- Speed with the ball.

Relay game: played by two teams.
Playing area: the midfield circle.

Some cones are placed along the midfield circle, at a distance of 2-3 yards from each other.

A cone-marked 5-6 yard square is in the center.

The two teams form a line along the midfield line, with the first player close to the circle. One player (O) from each team is placed inside the square.

When the coach gives the signal, players O pass the ball to the first player of their respective teams and quickly run to the back of the line. At the same time, the first player of each team goes to the ball, turns and dribbles it in the same direction, slaloming through the cones placed on the circle.

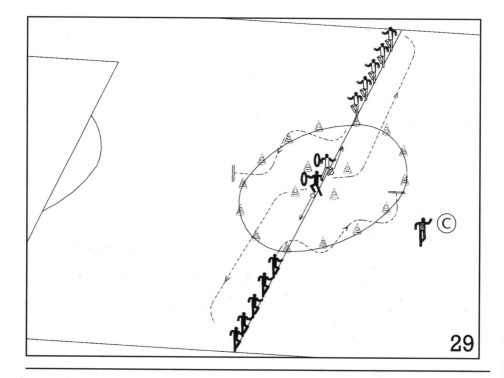

29

After he has dribbled the ball all around the circle he goes to the square, turns around a cone, passes the ball to the first teammate and goes to the back of the line. The exercise goes on like this for all the players: receiving, turning, dribbling and passing, until all of them have carried it out. The winner is the team who finishes first, or that is the first to reach the established number of goes.

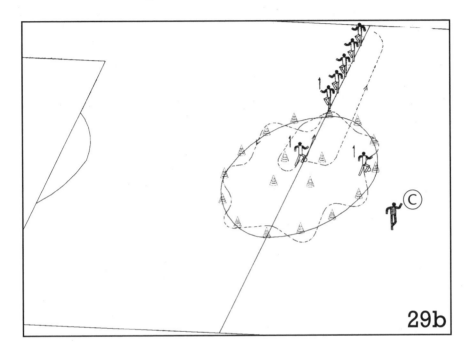

29b

COACHING POINTS

Dribbling:
- Kick the ball with the part of the inside or outside of the foot which is closer to the tip;
- The foot pushes the ball;
- The foot must be turned as soon as it kicks the ball: it touches the ground again with the sole, as when running;
- The kicking foot is about 2 inches from the ground;
- Coach one foot at a time;
- With the outside of the right foot, clockwise;
- With the inside of the left foot, clockwise;
- With the outside of the left foot, counterclockwise;
- With the inside of the right foot, counterclockwise;
- As for turning from the center of the field to the circle see **GAME 26**;
- As for turning around the cone see **GAME 28**.

GAME 30

OBJECTIVE

- Ability to turn and pass.
- Turn and dribble the ball along a circle.
- Speed with the ball.

This game is a variation of game 29.
If you wish to develop endurance, the game can be played with two balls.
   Two players (O1 and O2) from each team are placed inside the cone-marked square in the center; each of them has a ball.
   When the coach gives the signal, players O1 pass the ball to the first player of their respective teams (A) and quickly run to the back of the line.
Players A go to the ball, turn and dribble it in the same direction, slaloming through the cones placed on the circle.

Players O2 and B start their exercise exactly when players A start slaloming with the ball through the cones. They carry out the same exercise as O1 and A.

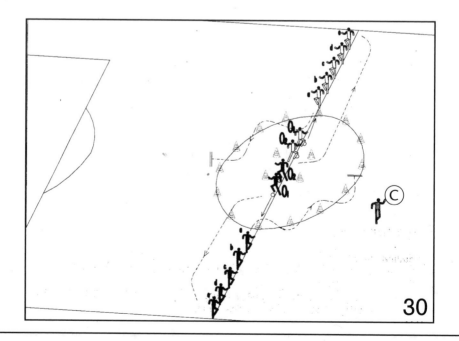

30

After dribbling all around the circle, players A go to the square, turn around a cone, pass the ball to player C and go to the back of the line. Players C carry out the same exercise with the next teammates, and so on. The exercise finishes when all the players have carried it out.

The winner is the team who finishes first, or that is the first to reach the established number of goes.

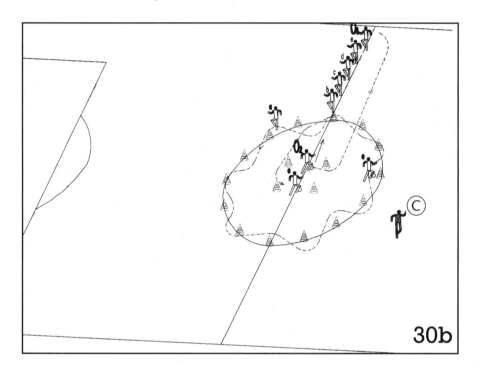

30b

COACHING POINTS

Dribbling:
- Kick the ball with the part of the inside or outside of the foot which is closer to the tip;
- The foot pushes the ball;
- The foot must be turned as soon as it kicks the ball: it touches the ground again with the sole, as when running;
- The kicking foot is about 2 inches from the ground;
- Coach one foot at a time;
- With the outside of the right foot, clockwise;
- With the inside of the left foot, clockwise;
- With the outside of the left foot, counterclockwise;
- With the inside of the right foot, counterclockwise;
- As for turning from the center of the field to the circle see GAME 26;
- As for turning around the cone see GAME 28.

GAME 31

OBJECTIVE

- Developing the ability to play with superiority in numbers.
- Getting used to seeing the teammate free from marking.
- Getting used to immediately spotting the opponent to challenge or to mark.

Team game: played by 2 teams.

Playing area: form some cone-marked rectangles with a hurdle in the middle to be used as a small goal.

This game is played by groups of five players made up of two players from one team and three from the other..

The team with superiority in numbers attacks the small goal while the other team defends it.

The attacking players cannot enter the rectangle.

When the defenders win the ball they pass it to each other outside the rectangle.

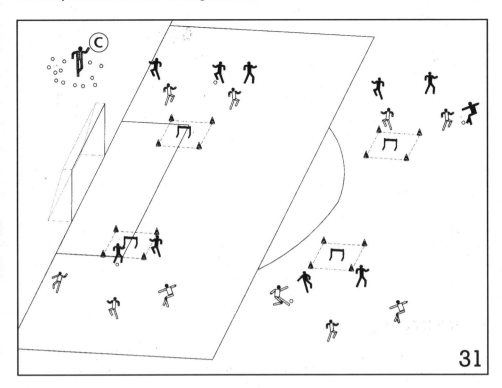

31

COACHING POINTS

After a certain time change the players' roles.
Ask the players to volley-pass the ball.

GAME 32

OBJECTIVE

- Accurate passes.
- Shots with the inside of the instep by the players to the attackers.
- Ability to turn.
- Shots at goal from outside the penalty area.

Team game: played by 2 teams.

Form a line of flags parallel to the edge of the penalty area at a distance of 10 yards. The distances between the flags should be 5-6 yards.

The team in black is divided in two groups (**A** and **B**). The players of group A have each got a ball and are positioned opposite the goal and the flags. Group **B** is placed inside the penalty area. The team in white is positioned in "zone **K**", in front of group **A**.

Groups **A** and **B** pass the ball to each other: group **A** with low-ground passes through the flags, group B with high clearances with the inside of the instep. When the players in white intercept the low passes from players A they turn with the ball and shoot at goal from outside the penalty area.

One or more players in white retrieve the ball after wide shots. Then coach should set a time limit, at the end of which the roles are reversed: the winner is the team that scores more goals.

COACHING POINTS

Ability to turn: see GAME 26.

The low, direct pass can be made with the inside of the foot or with the instep.

1. **Kicking the ball with the inside of the instep (defenders):**
- kick the ball with the part of the foot just under the shoe-strings;
- the supporting foot is sideways to the ball, distant from it;
- the run-up is diagonal;
- the tip of the kicking foot nearly scrapes the ground.

2. **Shooting from outside the penalty area with the inside of the instep, making the ball rotate:**
- the run-up is a 45-degree diagonal;
- the supporting foot is slightly behind and sideways to the ball;

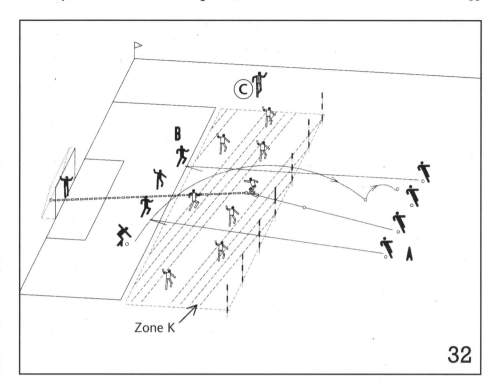

Zone K

32

- slightly rotate the hip and the knee outward;
- the tiptoes of the kicking foot are slightly raised;
- the ball must be kicked below the middle and with the inside of the big toe, then of the foot;
- the kicking leg follows the ball.

3. **Shooting from outside the penalty area with the outside of the foot, making the ball rotate:**
- the run-up is diagonal, starting from the side of the kicking foot;
- the supporting foot is slightly behind and sideways to the ball;
- the kicking leg is slightly rotated inward;
- the upper body is bent to the supporting leg;
- the ball must be kicked below the middle with the outside of the tip and then with the part of the foot between the joint and the ankle;
- the kicking leg follows the ball.

GAME 33

OBJECTIVE

- Shots from outside the penalty area.

Team game: played by 2 teams.
Playing area: half field, with one goal.
The teams are arranged in the middle. When the coach whistles, the goal-keeper returns the ball and a regular soccer match is played, with a variation: the players cannot enter the penalty area.

Each team tries to score goals with shots from outside the penalty area.

The winner is either the team which scores more goals or the team with the higher number of scoring players.

COACHING POINTS

1. Low-ground shots:
- the supporting foot is sideways to the ball;
- the body is bent forward;
- when the ball is kicked the knee of the kicking foot is over the ball;
- the ball is kicked in the middle;
- stretch out the knee soon after kicking;

2. Sideways volley kick:
- the body is placed in a right angle with regard to the ball;
- the kicking leg is at hip's height, with a semicircular movement to the ball;
- kick the ball with the instep, arms open outward;

3. Shooting with the outside of the foot, making the ball rotate:
- the run-up is diagonal, starting from the side of the kicking foot;
- the supporting foot is slightly behind and sideways to the ball;
- the kicking leg is slightly rotated inward;
- the upper body is bent to the supporting leg;
- the ball must be kicked below the middle with the outside of the tip and then with the part of the foot between the joint and the ankle;
- the kicking leg follows the ball.

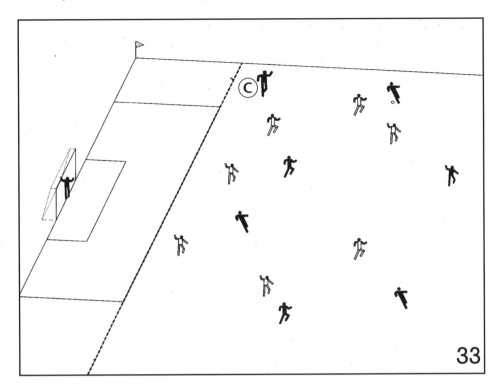

4. Shooting with the inside of the instep, making the ball rotate:
- the supporting foot is slightly behind and sideways to the ball;
- slightly rotate the hip and the knee outward;
- the tiptoes of the kicking foot are slightly raised;
- the ball must be kicked below the middle and with the inside of the big toe, then of the foot;
- the kicking leg follows the ball.

GAME 34

OBJECTIVE

- Shots at goal from outside the penalty area.
- Crosses.
- Headers on crosses.

This game is a variation of game 33.
One or more players of each team are arranged inside the penalty area, playing as attackers and defenders.

Without getting out of the penalty area, the attackers build up chances to score a goal with the outside teammates, who pass them the ball. So, the inside players try to score on a cross or deep pass from their outside teammates, while the latter can shoot at goal only from outside the penalty area.

The defenders try to intercept the passes.

A point is scored when a pass is intercepted.

A goal scores two points.

At the end of the time limit the roles are reversed.

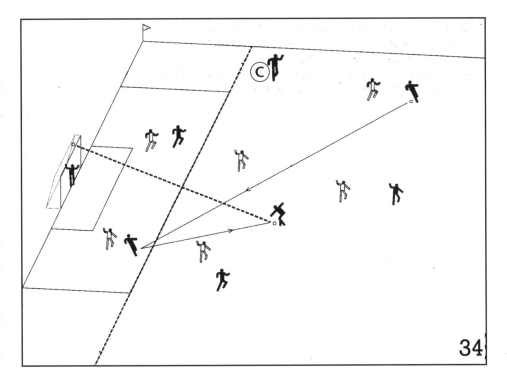

COACHING POINTS

1. **Shooting from the outside of the penalty area with the inside of the instep, making the ball rotate:**
- the run-up is a 45-degree diagonal;
- the supporting foot is slightly behind and sideways to the ball;
- slightly rotate the hip and the knee outward;
- the tiptoes of the kicking foot are slightly raised;
- the ball must be kicked below the middle and with the inside of the big toe, then of the foot;
- the kicking leg follows the ball.

2. **Shooting from outside the penalty area with the with the outside of the foot, making the ball rotate:**
- the run-up is diagonal, starting from the side of the kicking foot;
- the supporting foot is slightly behind and sideways to the ball;
- the kicking leg is slightly rotated inward;
- the upper body is bent to the supporting leg;
- the ball must be kicked below the middle with the outside of the tip and then with the part of the foot between the joint and the ankle;
- the kicking leg follows the ball.

GAME 35

OBJECTIVE

- Low-ground hard shots with the instep.
- Speed off the ball.
- Preliminary exercise for diving headers.

Team game: played by 2 teams.
Playing area: the penalty area.
The players in black try to hit those in white with the ball.

Place three flags 2-3 yards inside one of the penalty area sidelines. Tie a tape between the flags at a height of 1-1.5 yards. Along a parallel line to the tape, at a distance of 4-5 yards, place as many balls as the players of the black team. The distance between the balls should be 2-3 yards. Near the other sideline of the penalty area place as many hurdles as players in white. The players in black are outside the penalty area, at a distance of 7-8 yards from the balls; those in white are 5-6 yards beyond the tape, sitting with their backs to the opponents.

When the coach gives the signal, the players in black start running and each of them kicks the ball with the instep, making it pass under the tape and trying to hit the players in white. At the same time the latter get up and, without getting out of the penalty area, quickly run to the hurdles and dive over them after pushing on one foot (less advanced players can pass under the hurdle on all fours).

The players in black score a point when they hit a player in white; then, they retrieve the ball and put it back to the starting place.
The roles are reversed after an established number of goes.

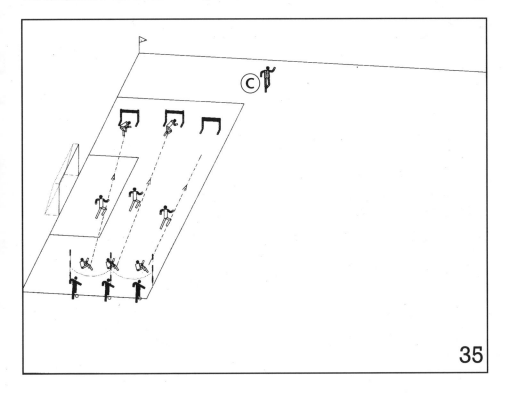

35

COACHING POINTS

1. For low-ground shots:
- the run-up must be perpendicular to the ball;
- cast a glance to see the position of the target;
- the eyes must kept on the ball when the foot is getting ready to shoot;
- the last step must be longer;
- the supporting foot is sideways to the ball;
- the kicking foot is stretched out with the tip downward and the ball is kicked with the instep;
- when the ball is kicked, the supporting foot raises and the head is perpendicular to the ball (in this way it is easier to obtain a low trajectory);
- the leg follows the ball after the kick and the run continues for two or three steps.

2. Speed:
- give the players time to recover before the following sprint.

GAME 36

OBJECTIVE

- Low-ground hard shots with the instep while moving.
- Speed off the ball.

This game is a variation of game 35.
Scatter some cones and hurdles in the area near the tape, between the penalty area and the sideline.

The players in white each have a ball and are positioned on the sideline, near the cones and hurdles.

The players in black are inside the penalty area, sitting with their backs to the opponents at a distance of 2-3 yards from the tape.

When the coach gives the signal the players in white start dribbling through the obstacles to the tape. When the coach gives a second signal, the players in white kick the ball with the instep, making it pass under the tape and trying to hit the players in black. At the same time the latter get up and, without getting out of the penalty area, quickly run to the hurdles and dive over them after pushing on one foot.

The players in white score a point when they hit a player in black; then, they retrieve the ball and put it back to the starting place.

The roles are reversed after an established number of goes.

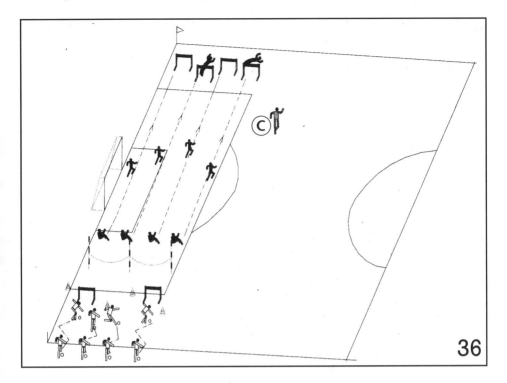

COACHING POINTS

1. For shots:
- the supporting foot is a bit ahead of the ball and very close to it;
- cast a glance to see the position of the target;
- the eyes must kept on the ball when the foot is getting ready to shoot;
- the last step must be longer;
- the ball must be kicked in the middle;
- a moment before the kick, the supporting leg slightly bends;
- the movement of the kicking leg starts from the hip with the knee bent;
- the kicking foot is stretched out and kicks the ball with the part under the shoe-strings;
- when the ball is kicked, the supporting foot raises and the head is over the ball;
- the leg follows the ball after the kick and the run continues for two or three steps.

2. Speed:
- do not speed up the ball retrieval, give the players time to recover before the following sprint.

GAME 37

OBJECTIVE

- Quickness, readiness.
- Headers.

Team game: played by 2 teams.
Playing area: the penalty area with its goal.
Just outside the edge of the six yard area three flags are placed with a tape tied between them: the distance between them should be greater than the depth of the six yard area. The players from both teams are arranged 6-7 yards beyond the tape, along the edge of the penalty area: they are lying on their backs (or sitting) with their arms up and a ball in their hands. The two teams are about 3 yards from each other and each player has a number.

The coach calls out a number, 1: players number 1 throw the ball upward and forward, then quickly get up and with a header above the tape try to score a goal.

Each goal scores a point.

If both players score a goal the point is given to the player who scored first.

After a certain number of headers it is better to change the teams' positions.

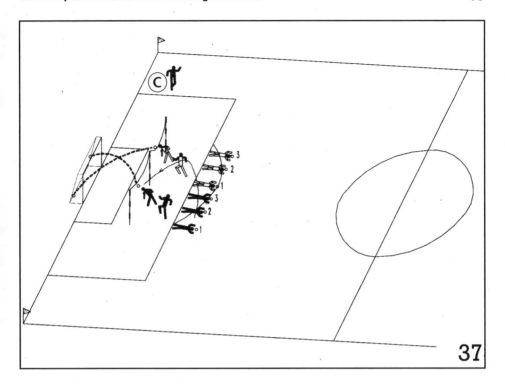

COACHING POINTS

Give the players time to recover before the following sprint.

For headers:
- take-off on only one foot;
- the taking-off leg pushes upward;
- the last step must be longer;
- the upper body bends and pushes forward;
- head the ball either with the center or the sides of the forehead;
- the neck muscles are tense during the header.

GAME 38

OBJECTIVE

- Quickness, readiness.
- Diving headers.

This game is a variation of game 37.
The players are standing with a ball in their hands.

The coach calls out a number, 1: players number 1 throw the ball up behind the tape with their hands or they kick it there with the instep, then they quickly run and with a diving header below the tape try to score a goal.

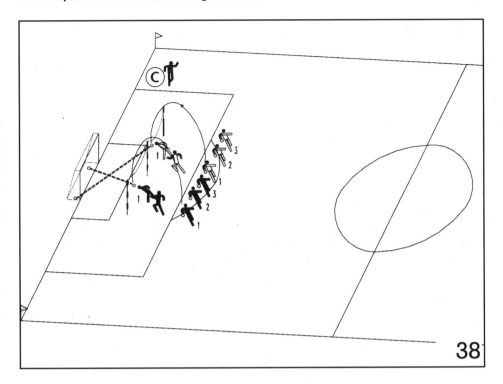

COACHING POINTS

Give the players time to recover before the following sprint.

Diving headers:
- the last step must be longer;
- take-off on only one foot (standing jumps are less effective and do not provide for a good balance, while a greater forward push is achieved by taking-off on only one foot);
- the tip of the foot of the taking-off leg pushes forward;
- while the taking-off leg pushes the other one rises;
- head the ball with the forehead;
- land on the palms of the hands, cushioning with the arms.

GAME 39

OBJECTIVE

- Quickness, readiness.
- Back header.

Team game: played by 2 teams.

Playing area: the penalty area with the goal divided into three parts by two flags, with different score: the central part is wider so it has a smaller score. A line of flags is placed along the edge of the six yard area. The distance between them is 3-4 yards and this line is longer than the line of the edge.

The players from both teams are arranged at a distance of 2-3 yards from the flags, with their backs to the goal. Each player has a number and has a ball in his hands.

The coach calls out a number, 1: players number 1 throw the ball upward with their hands or they kick it upwards with the instep, then with a back header they make the ball go beyond the flags. They immediately turn around, sprint to the ball and shoot at goal after it has bounced.

Each goal scores the points of the goal section it goes through.

After a certain number of headers the position of the two teams should be reversed.

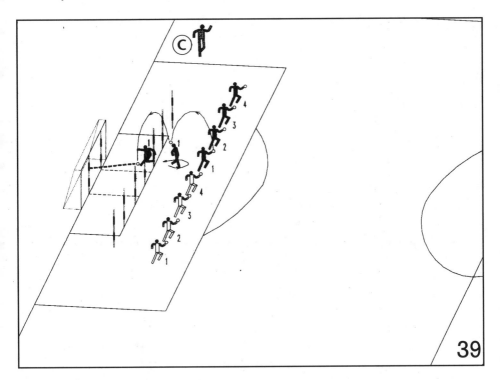

39

COACHING POINTS

Give the players time to recover before the following sprint.

Back headers:
- place yourself under the ball;
- forehead up;
- head the ball with the upper part of the forehead keeping the head backward;
- Slightly bend the legs while the ball comes down;
- the header is accompanied by the extension of the legs.

GAME 40

OBJECTIVE

• Quickness, readiness.
• Accurate shots when the ball is moving.

Team game: played by 2 teams.

Playing area: with a line of flags form irregular goals, each with a different score. The two teams, 3-4 yards from each other, form a line at a distance of 15-20 yards from the flags. Each player is numbered and has a ball in his hands. A teammate (A) is placed opposite each team, at a distance of 6-7 yards: he has several balls and has the task of passing the ball.

The coach calls out a number, 1: the players with that number throw their ball upward with their hands (or they kick it upwards with the instep). At the same time, players A pass a ball to them and they volley-kick it through one of the goals with the inside of the foot; then they quickly turn and catch their ball before it touches the ground. After they have caught their ball they retrieve the one they have kicked and give it back to player A, who after a certain number of goes is replaced by a teammate.

Each shot scores the points of the goal the ball goes through:

• of course the ball thrown upward with the hands must not touch the ground or the shot will not count.

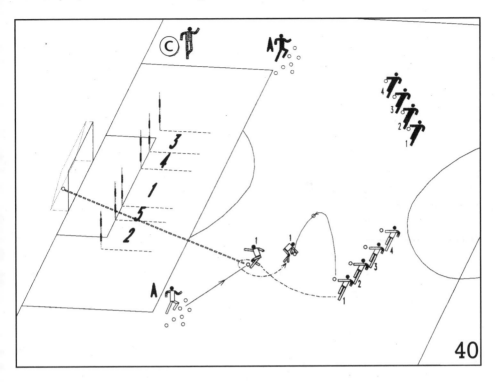

COACHING POINTS

Player A should pass the ball to the right or to the left of his teammate.

Kicking the ball with the inside of the foot:
- the run must be perpendicular to the ball;
- the last step must be slightly longer;
- the ball must be kicked when it is along the same line as the supporting foot;
- the ball must be kicked in the middle;
- the kicking foot is 2 inches above the ground;
- the kicking foot follows the ball.

GAME 41

OBJECTIVE

- Quickness, readiness.
- Ball control.

Team game: played by 2 teams.

Playing area: two flags are placed at a distance of 10 yards from each other and connected with a tape. The teams are arranged in two lines, 5-6 yards from the tape.

When the coach gives the signal, the first player of each line places the sole of the foot on the ball and, with a slight retroaction, makes the ball roll backward on the upper part of his foot. As soon as the ball starts moving he softly shoots it forward over the tape. Then he quickly runs forward under the tape and gets the ball on the other side, turns with it to the side and slaloms through a line of cones, passes it to the next teammate and goes to the back of the line.

The exercise goes on until each player has had a go.

The winner is the team to finish the established number of goes first.

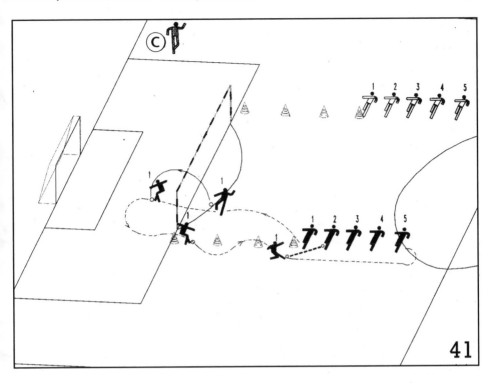

COACHING POINTS

Ball control:
- place the tip of the foot under the ball;
- carry out the exercise with both feet;
- the sole of the foot must be placed softly on the ball.

GAME 42

OBJECTIVE

- Quickness, readiness.
- Feints.

Individual game.

Form a 7-8 yard square with four cones. Place one player behind each cone and one player (A) in the center with a ball. Player A dribbles the ball to one of the players behind the cones, then makes a feint and dribbles it to another teammate; when he is close, he makes another feint and so forth. While player A is going from one teammate to the other after the feint, the four players quickly exchange their places with one another: Player A tries to take advantage of this, leaving the ball and running to occupy one of his teammates' place. Player A's game has a time limit: he scores a point each time he occupies one place.

When the time is over another player carries out the exercise. The game finishes when all the players have played the role of A: the winner is the one with the highest score.

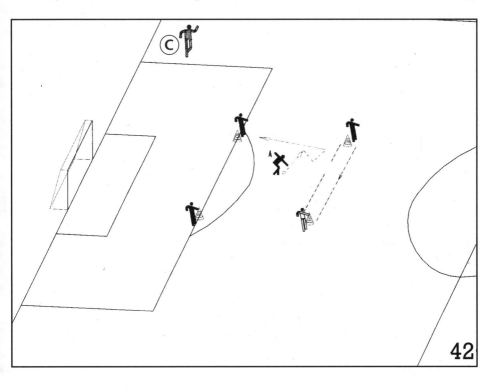

COACHING POINTS

Player A retrieves the ball slowly, so as to recover and be ready for the next sprints.

GAME 43

OBJECTIVE

- Quickness, readiness.
- Improvement of elevation.
- Preliminary exercise to take-off for headers.
- Shooting with the instep.

Team game: played by 2 teams.
Playing area: the midfield circle. Form as many cone-marked triangles as players in black on the circumference.
The black team is positioned in a circle inside the midfield circle; the players in white are in the center with their backs to the players in black and a ball.

The players in black are the target which those in white try to hit.

When the coach gives the signal, the players in black quickly run to their own triangle, take off on only one foot and jump into it, landing with feet close together.

At the same time the players in white shoot at them by kicking the ball with the instep, trying to hit them before they jump into their triangle. Each player then retrieves his own ball.

A point is scored when an opponent is hit.

After an established number of goes the roles are reversed.

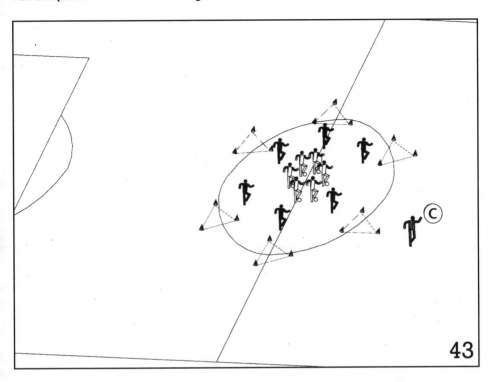

43

COACHING POINTS

Do not speed up the retrieval of the balls: the muscles relax, the heart-beat decreases and so the players are ready for the next sprints.

1. Jumps:
- The last step is longer;
- The weight is on the take-off leg;
- When taking-off, the other leg's knee is bent and is at the height of the waist;
- The arms are forward when the body is in the air.

2. Shots:
- Kick the ball with the part of the foot under the shoe strings;
- After the kick, the leg follows the ball and the run continues for two or three steps.

GAME 44

OBJECTIVE

- Quickness, readiness.
- Accurate passes.
- Shots at goal.

Team game: played by 2 teams.

Playing area: a 10 x 20-yard cone-marked area (for 20 players) with two goals. Draw a rectangle in front of each goal, slightly wider than the goals and 2 yards long, to be defended by the goalkeepers. In the playing area form as many cone-marked triangles as players: the distance between the triangles should be about 3 yards.

The two teams are arranged along the same line, starting from a distance of 5-6 yards from the sidelines.

When the coach gives the signal all the players sprint to occupy one of the triangles: if two or more players occupy the same triangle he who arrived first is allowed to remain, the other moves to another triangle.

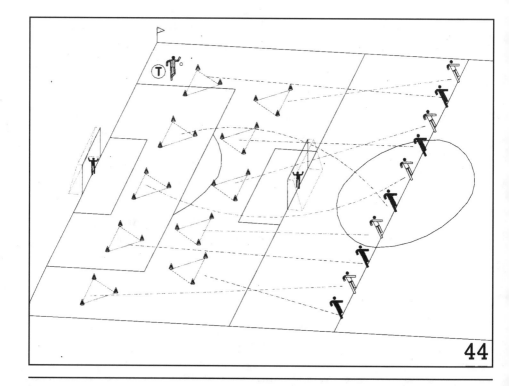

44

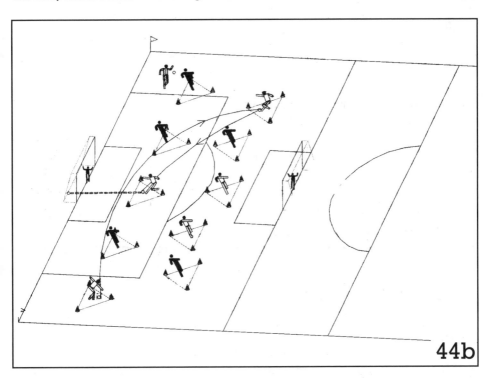

44b

At this moment the coach throws the ball into the field. The players pass it to one another or shoot at goal without getting out of their triangle. The ball can be hit with any part of the body, except the hands. If a player gets out of his triangle or touches the ball with his hands, the coach gives the ball to the closest opponent. After a shot at goal the teams go back to the starting position to do the exercise again.

The winner is the team that has scored more after an established number of goes.

COACHING POINTS

The distance between the triangles to be occupied and the starting point must be adapted to the children.

If there are slower children, establish that those who are last on the triangles will start some yards ahead of the others in the next sprints.

GAME 45

OBJECTIVE

- Quickness, readiness to anticipate the opponent and free oneself from marking.
- Making oneself available.
- High shots with the inside of the instep.

Team game: played by 2 teams.

This game is a kind of "prisoner ball".

The playing area is a 20 x 10 yard cone-marked rectangle, whose dimensions can be adapted to the number of players. The rectangle is like a volleyball court, divided in two halves with flags and a tape. The teams are arranged opposite each other.

When the coach whistles, one team starts serving: one player in black on the edge of the playing area kicks the ball over the tape to the other side after receiving a pass with the inside of the instep from a teammate. If the ball is touched with any part of the body (except the hands) by a player in white then the one in black who has kicked it is made prisoner and goes to the opposing field. He will be free again when he intercepts a ball kicked by a teammate before it touches the ground. Instead, if the kicked ball touches the ground before anybody can touch it, a player in white is made prisoner (or a prisoner in black is set free). A player is made prisoner when he kicks the ball out of the field.

Then the team in white serves, and so forth.

The winner is the team with more prisoners at the end.

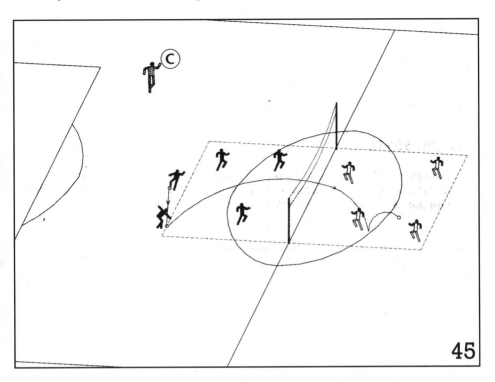

45

COACHING POINTS

High shots with the instep:

- The run-up should make a 45-degree angle in relation to the shooting direction;
- The supporting leg is bent and sideways to the ball;
- Slightly rotate the knee, hip and toes of the kicking leg outward (the toes are slightly raised);
- The upper body is tilted to the side of the supporting leg;
- Kick the ball with the inside of the foot; the kicking leg follows it.

GAME 46

OBJECTIVE

- Quickness of reflexes;
- Higher tension and intensity when fewer players.

Individual game.
Team game: played by 2 teams.
Playing area: a 6-7 x 4-5 yard cone-marked rectangle similar to a small volleyball court, with a goal at each end and divided in two halves with flags and a tape.

The players are divided in groups of three.

The players of each group play 2 versus 1, with a ball on both sides of the field. The game starts when the two sides kick the ball over the tape at the same time. The players try to score a goal with any part of the body (except the hands) by shooting over or under the tape.

The ball must be volleyed or kicked after one bounce. In turn each player plays alone.

The goes have a time limit.

The winner is the player with the highest score: the score is made up of the difference between the number of his and his opponents' goals when playing alone.

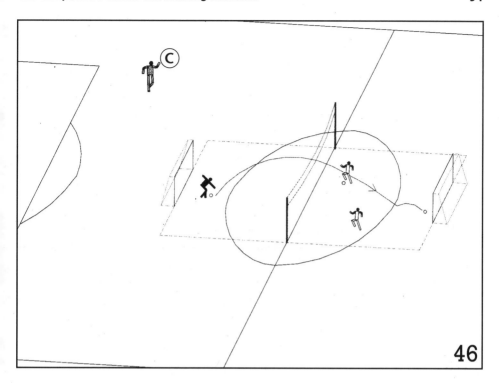

46

COACHING POINTS

When the ball goes out it is retrieved slowly.
The length of the goes must be adapted to the players' age.
The exercise can be done with only one ball if the players have difficulties.

GAME 47

OBJECTIVE

- Accurate shots.
- Speed of performance.

Team game: played by 2 teams.

Playing area: in the middle of the penalty area mark a rectangle (A) with paint and put many medicine balls into it. Sideways to the rectangles longer lines, form two small areas by tracing two lines that cannot be passed and place a team into each of them. Each player must have a ball. When the coach gives the signal, all the players shoot at the medicine balls in order to make them go out of "A" and roll into the opponents' area. The players retrieve the opponents' balls and kick them back.

Each team has a player (B and B1) who, on all fours, can take back to rectangle A the medicine balls rolled into his area and who can pass his teammates the balls in rectangle A. When players B and B1 are hit they are penalized with a run around the field.

When the coach stops the game, the players count the medicine balls on the respective areas. One point is scored by the team with fewer of them. Then the medicine balls are re-arranged in rectangle A, players B and B1 are replaced and a new game is played. The winner is the team that reaches the established score first.

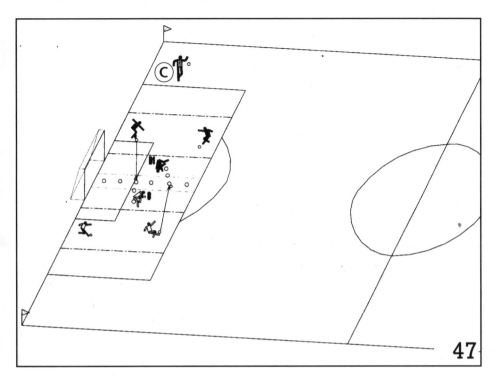

47

COACHING POINTS

When shooting, the supporting foot is near the ball with the tip in the direction of the target.
The kicking leg follows the ball.

GAME 48

OBJECTIVE

- Quickness of reflexes.
- Control of the ball
- Headers.

Individual game.

Playing area: a 6-7 x 3-4 yard cone-marked rectangle similar to a small volleyball court, divided in two halves with flags and a tape. The players are divided in pairs and each of them is placed opposite the other in his respective side of the field.

The ball is in the hands of one player who kicks it with the instep and then heads it over the tape, trying to make the ball reach as far as possible from the opponent (but not out of the field). After the ball has bounced, the opponent kicks it with the instep and then heads it back over the tape; he can also head it before the bounce or control it with the instep, chest or thigh, then kick it with the instep and head it back over the tape.

The game goes on like this until an established score is reached.

A player scores one point when the ball bounces more than once in the opposing field, when the opponent touches it with his hand or when the opponent kicks it outside.

The winner is the player who reaches the established score first.

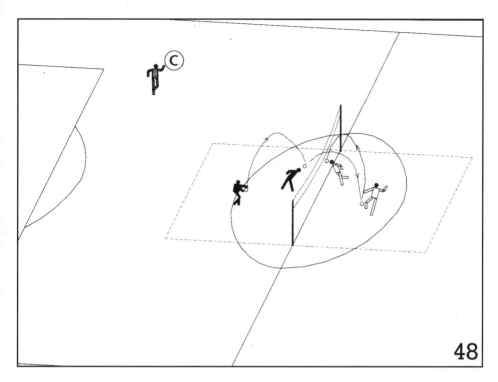

48

COACHING POINTS

When controlling the ball the instep is outstretched.

When heading the ball, take-off on only one foot and head the ball with the center, left or right of the forehead.

The game can be intensified by using two balls.

GAME 49

OBJECTIVE

- Speed of performance.
- Preliminary exercise to shots with the instep.
- Speed/Endurance.
- Getting to know one another.

Individual game.
Playing area: the midfield circle. The players are arranged in the midfield line around their teammate A, who has a ball.

The coach gives the signal by calling out the name of a player (B). A has the ball in his hands and immediately kicks it upward with the instep.

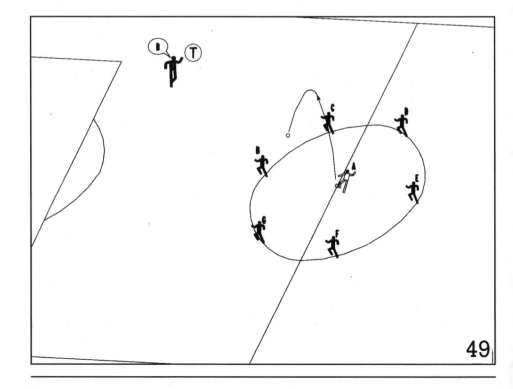

49

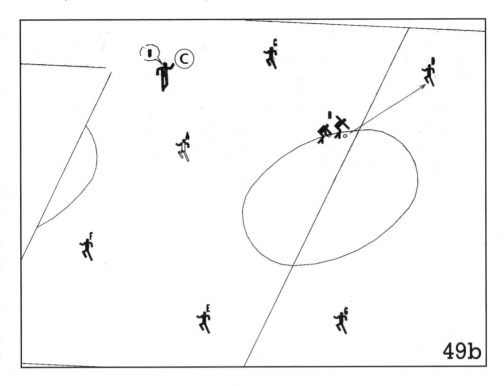

49b

B runs to the ball while A and the other players start running without getting outside the playing area. Once B catches the ball he runs after his teammates with it in his hands and tries to hit one by kicking it with the instep. B has 20 seconds to hit the other players. If he does not hit any he goes back to the center of the playing area and starts the game again; instead, if he hits a teammate the latter restarts the game.

One point is scored every time a player is hit. The winner is the player who reaches the established score first.

COACHING POINTS

This game is ideal for a gymnasium.
When shooting with the instep the ball must be kicked with the part of the foot which is under the shoe strings; the kicking leg follows the ball.

GAME 50

OBJECTIVE

• More balls provide for higher tension and intensity.

Team game: played by 2 teams.

Playing area: the Playing area is a 20 x 10 yard cone-marked rectangle, whose dimensions can be adapted to the number of players. The rectangle is like a volleyball court, divided in two halves with flags and a tape. The teams are arranged opposite each other.

Each player has a ball.

When the coach whistles, each player sends the ball over the tape. The ball can be sent with any part of the body, except the hands. The balls can be sent back by volley, after one or more bounces and also from a dead ball position.

When the ball is sent outside the opposing field the player who has kicked it quickly goes and retrieves it, then runs back to his own field and kicks it again.

When the coach stops the game the players count the balls in their field.

The team with fewer balls in its field scores a point.

The game goes on like this until the established score is reached.

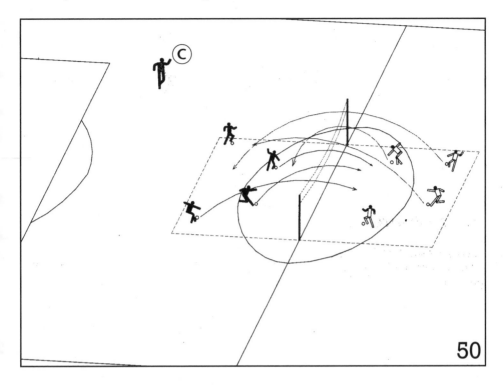

50

COACHING POINTS

This game is ideal for a gymnasium.
Allow the players to recover after stopping the game.
As a variation, the ball can be sent under the tape.

GAME 51

OBJECTIVE

- Quickness of reflexes.
- Speed of performance - speed endurance.
- Accurate shots.
- Controlling the ball with the inside of the foot.
- Dribbling.

Team game: played by 2 teams.
Playing area: the playing area is a 20 x 10 yard cone-marked rectangle, whose dimensions can be adapted to the number of players. The rectangle is like a volleyball court, divided in two halves with flags and a tape one yard above the ground. Trace an inner line at a distance of 5-6 yards from the midfield line in order to form areas A and A1 (shooting areas), as shown in the diagram. Scatter objects of various size on the perimeter: plastic glasses and bottles, piles of cones, bags and drinking cans one on top of the other in the shape of a pyramid: the bigger the object, the lower the score (e.g. a plastic cup scores 5 points, while a pyramid of bags 1). The teams are arranged opposite each other, outside areas A-A1. Each player has a ball.

When the coach gives the signal, the players dribble the ball to their respective shooting area and shoot below the tape trying to hit the opposing targets. They retrieve the ball and start again: they dribble the ball to A-A1 and then shoot. They can shoot only from areas A-A1, but cannot remain there: if they do they are penalized.

When the coach stops the game the players count their points according to the targets they have hit; then they re-arrange the objects and play again.

The game ends when a team reaches the established score first.

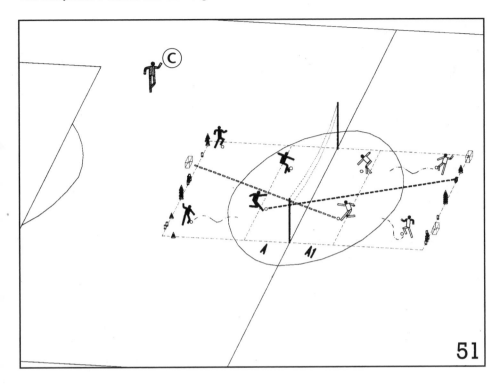

51

COACHING POINTS

This game is ideal for a gymnasium.

Ask the players not to place themselves too close to the shooting area so as to move to the opponents' balls and control them better.

When the ball is controlled with the inside of the foot the controlling leg must not be stiff: first it must be moved forward and then backward just a moment before it touches the ball, so that the ball contacts the leg while it is moving in the same direction.

GAME 52

OBJECTIVE

- Immediate shot at goal with a sudden sprint.
- The triangles around the circumference help put spin on the ball.
- Quickness of reflexes.
- Speed of movement.
- Stimulation of coordination for shooting at goal: the round surface of the garbage can gives the ball less predictable trajectories.

Team game: played by 2 teams.

Playing area: place two inclined benches inside the midfield circle, with one end on a chair or a bag. Place four small goals (hurdles) around the benches at a distance of 12-15 yards, as shown in the diagram. At a distance of 10-15 yards from the midfield circle (depending on the number of players) place small goals and benches in order to form 4, 12-15 yard triangles. Tie a garbage can to each bench. When the coach gives the signal, the player who has the ball in his hands starts passing it to his teammates. The passes can be made by kicks with the instep, drop-kicks or headers. Each player has a handkerchief hanging from his waist: when a player manages to pull it off from an opponent when the latter has the ball in his hands he wins the ball and can throw it in. A player can shoot at one of the small goals only after the ball has been thrown to the bench or the garbage can with the hands and has bounced back. The ball can be shot by volley or after a bounce with any part of the body, except the hands.

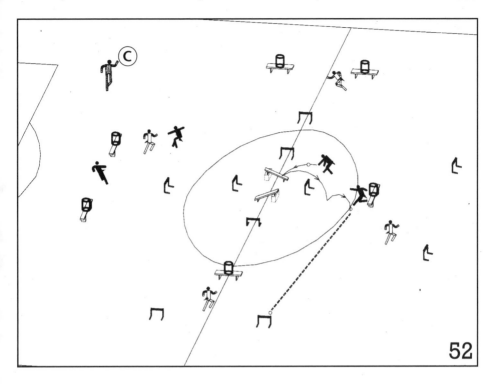

COACHING POINTS

Ask the players to look at where they want to shoot the ball before receiving it.

GAME 53

OBJECTIVE

• Shots at goal with a sudden sprint.

Team game: played by 2 teams.
Playing area: around the outside of the midfield circle place 4 small goals (hurdles) and 4 wooden triangles at a distance of 10-15 yards from each other, alternately.

When the coach gives the signal the teams play as in a match on a smaller field.

A ball can be shot at one of the small goals only by volley after it has been kicked to a triangle and has bounced back.

•   The winner is the team that scores more goals.

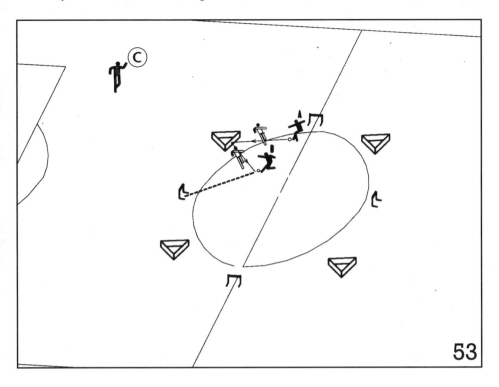

53

COACHING POINTS

Ask the players to shoot at the triangle from a distance of 5-6 yards.

GAME 54

OBJECTIVE

- Quickness - readiness.
- Shots at goal.

Team game: played by 2 teams.

The teams are arranged in a line, one on the left and the other on the right inside the penalty area. Each player is assigned a number and has a ball in his hands. A line of cones is placed on the edge of the penalty area.

The coach calls out a number, 7. Players 7 drop the ball from their hands and kick it upward with the instep. They quickly run to the edge of the penalty area, make a cone fall and quickly run back to the ball they kicked before, trying to shoot at goal.

A header scores 2 points.

The player who shoots first scores 1 point.

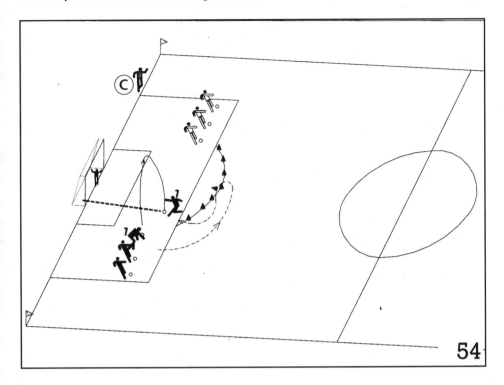

54

COACHING POINTS

After a certain number of shots at goal the positions of the teams and of the players in the line should be changed.

The distance between the cones and the players should be adapted to their abilities.

GAME 55

OBJECTIVE

- Headers.
- Ball control.
- Quickness of reflexes.

Team game: played by 2 teams.
Each team is divided in two groups: the team in black in groups A-A1, the team in white in groups B-B1. The penalty area is divided by a thick line of flags, acting as a net. Form cone-marked playing areas as shown in the diagram. Each group is placed in its respective area and has a ball. When the coach gives the signal, groups A and B send the ball over the net to their teammates by a header. The ball can be passed by volley, after a bounce or after three passes.

The opposing team scores a point when the ball bounces more than once, is intercepted by an opponent or is sent out of the field.

The winner is the team that reaches the established score first.

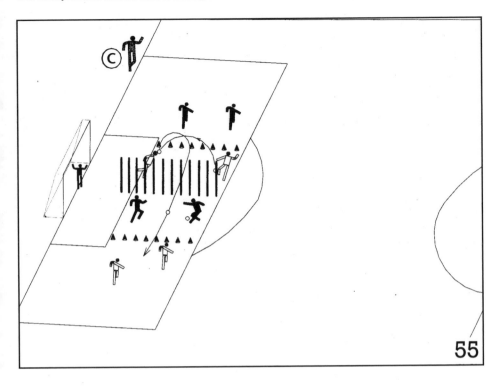

55

COACHING POINTS

The ball must be hit with the forehead.

GAME 56

OBJECTIVE

- Quickness of reflexes.
- Penetrating pass with the inside of the foot.

This game is a variation of game 55.
As shown in the diagram, the line of flags is substituted by a neutral area. When the coach gives the signal, groups A and B pass the ball to their teammates: the ball must cross the neutral area, where the players cannot enter.

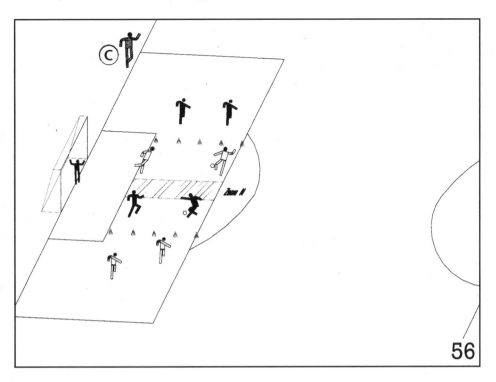

COACHING POINTS

In passes, the supporting foot is sideways to the ball while the kicking foot makes a right angle with the supporting foot; the kicking leg follows the ball.

GAME 57

OBJECTIVE

- Agility.
- Shots with the instep.

Individual game.

Playing area: the players are arranged along the midfield circle; in the center there is a fake wall (the one used to practice free kicks) with a player behind. The players are each assigned a number and have a ball in their hands: when the coach gives the signal, in turn they drop the ball and kick it with the instep after a bounce to hit the teammate placed near the fake wall. The latter must duck the shot by quickly changing position behind the wall. After shooting, the players retrieve their ball and go back to their position waiting for the next shot.

After an established length of time the player near the fake wall is repaced. The game is over when all the players have played as a target.

The winner is the player that has been hit the least.

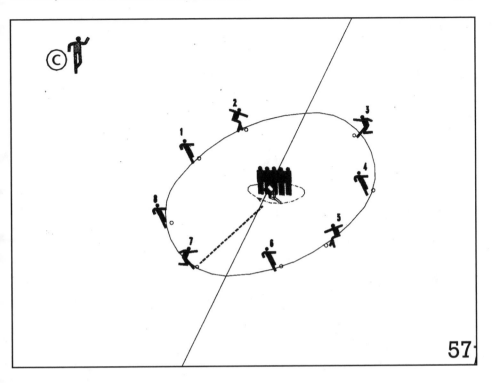

COACHING POINTS

When shooting, kick the ball with the part of the foot under the shoe-strings; the shooting leg follows the ball.

GAME 58

OBJECTIVE

- Speed - Agility.
- Feel for the body.
- Preliminary exercise to diving headers.

Team game: played by 2 teams.

Form two circuits with two flags each, to be used as starting and finishing posts. In between, place cones at a distance of 6-7 yards from one another. Each team forms a line in front of a circuit; the first player holds a ball in his hands.

When the coach gives the signal, the first player of each line drops the ball and kicks it upward with the instep, shooting it to the space between the first ranging rod and the first cone: then he quickly runs to the ball and dives under it after it has bounced. After that, he gets up, catches the ball and kicks it upward to the second space, then runs to the ball and dives under it after it has bounced, and so forth up to the finishing post; then he returns to the starting point, passes the ball to the next player and goes to the back of the line. The player who has received the ball does the same exercise and at the end passes it to the next teammate and so forth: the go finishes when all the players have finished the circuit.

The team whose players finish the exercise first wins the go; at the end the winner is the team that has won more goes.

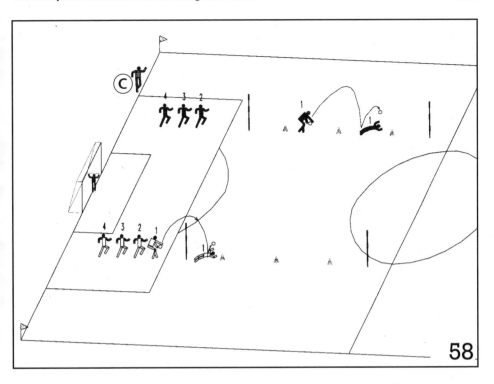

58

COACHING POINTS

Take-off on only one foot for diving.
The last step must be longer.

GAME 59

OBJECTIVE

- Speed/Endurance.
- Headers.

Team game: played by 2 teams.

The playing area is small, depending on the number of players. Each players has a ball in his hands and four or five clothes pegs inserted into the top front of his waist. The players try to hit each other with the ball by throwing it up and then heading it. When a player is hit he gives a clothes peg to the opponent. If a player loses all his clothes pegs he is eliminated. The team with the higher number of clothes pegs when the established time is over is the winner.

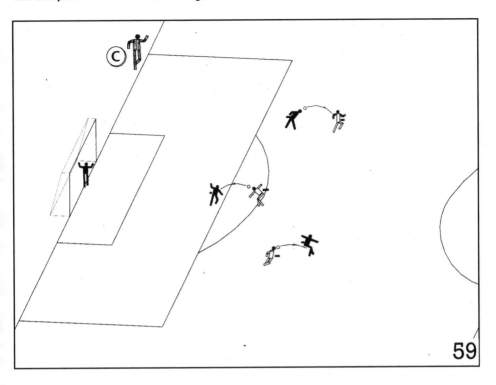

COACHING POINTS

Ask the players to throw up the ball 3-4 yards forward and then head it with the center of the forehead.

GAME 60

OBJECTIVE

- Speed/Endurance.
- Dribbling.
- Headers.

Team game: played by 2 teams.

Place several balls inside the midfield circle. The teams are sitting in a line, at a distance of 8-9 yards from each other and 25 yards from the balls. Place two flags with a tape (a kind of volleyball net) at a distance of about 10 yards from each team, as shown in the diagram. Between the balls and the tape form a line of cones, 2.5 yards from one another.

When the coach gives the signal, a player from each team quickly runs to the balls, picks one and slaloms with it through the cones. Then he catches it and heads it over the tape: after that he runs under the tape to the ball, dribbles it to a pre-established point, leaves it there and sits at the back of the line. As soon as he is sitting the next player can start and do the same exercise.

The go ends when the balls are finished and it is won by the team with the higher number of balls in the pre-established place.

At the end, the winner is the team that has won more goes.

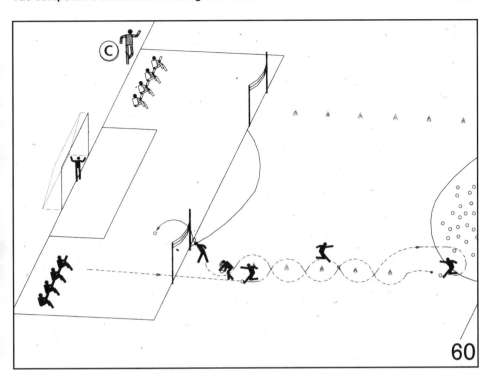

60

COACHING POINTS

Slalom through the cones at one touch, with the inside or the outside of the foot.

Head the ball with the forehead and take-off on only one foot.

Slowly re-arrange the balls for the next goes so that the players have time to recover.

GAME 61

OBJECTIVE

- Dribbling and feinting
- Headers.

This game is a variation of game 60.
The player kicks the ball over the tape in the following way: after dribbling through the cones, he controls it with the inside of the left foot. Then he spins as if he were going to turn left, places the sole of the left (or right) foot on the ball and, with a slight retroaction, makes the ball roll backward on the upper part of his foot. As soon as the ball starts moving he softly shoots it forward over the tape.

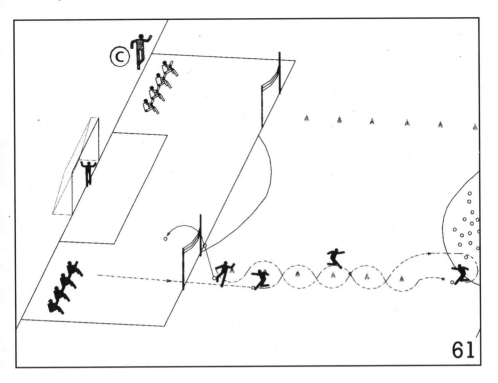

COACHING POINTS

Slalom through the cones with one touch, with the inside or the outside of the foot.

Head the ball with the forehead and take-off on only one foot.

Slowly re-arrange the balls for the next goes so that the players have time to recover.

GAME 62

OBJECTIVE

- Strengthening the muscles of the arms and of the upper body.
- Agility of the spine.
- Develop feel for the header.

Team game: played by 2 teams.

The two teams are divided in pairs and are arranged opposite each other on the sidelines of the penalty area. Each pair has a ball; one player of each pair walks on his hands while the other holds him by his ankles. The players walking on their hands push the ball forward with their head. The teams cross the penalty area like this until they reach the opposite side. The winner is the team whose players are on the opposite side first.

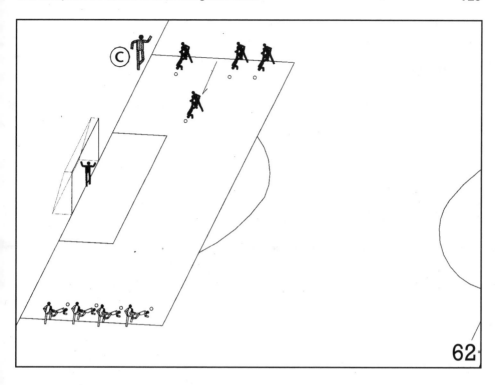

COACHING POINTS

Ask the players to keep their pelvis along the same line as their upper body.

The back must not be arched too much.

GAME 63

OBJECTIVE

- Strengthening the muscles of the arms and of the upper body.
- Agility of the spine.
- Develop feel for the header.

This game is a variation of game 62.

The players of the two teams are on all fours and are arranged opposite each other on the sidelines of the penalty area.

When the coach gives the signal, each player pushes the ball forward with his forehead up to the opposite side.

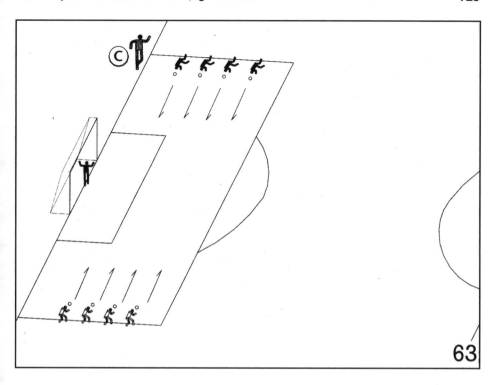

63

COACHING POINTS

Ask the players to keep their pelvis along the same line as their upper body.

The back must not be arched too much.

GAME 64

OBJECTIVE

- Control of the ball.

This game is played on a very small field, depending on the number of players. The players are divided in pairs: one pair is blindfolded while the others each have a ball. Prepare a kind of "hammer" by putting a ball into a towel and joining its four corners. The two "hammers" will be used by the blindfolded players, who are placed near the sides of the playing area. The other players are scattered in the field as they please. When the coach gives the signal, the blindfolded players start walking around while whirling their "hammer" in order to hit the other players, who meanwhile are moving while carrying out an exercise (they let the ball bounce and kick it with the outstretched instep).

The coach can give directions to the blindfolded pair.

When the blindfolded players hit another player they score a point. The go has a time limit.

Play as many goes as there are pairs.

The winner is the pair with the highest score.

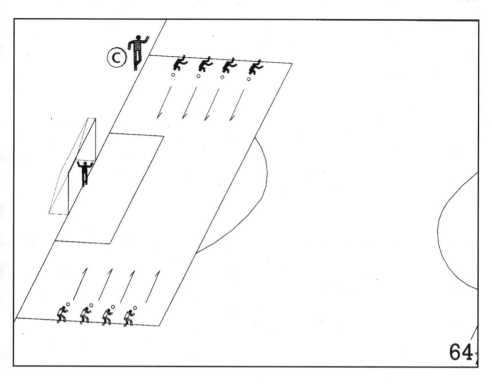

COACHING POINTS

Kick the ball with the outstretched foot parallel to the ground.

GAME 65

OBJECTIVE

• Speed/Endurance

Team Game: Played by 2 teams.

Just outside the midfield circle, form a line with as many hurdles or flags as players of a team. The players in white sit in a line in the midfield circle with their backs to the hurdles. One player in black sits with them while the others wait for the end of the go outside the playing area.

The game starts when one player in white goes in front of his teammates, drops the ball from his hands and performs an overhead kick trying to shoot the ball as far as possible. All the players in white (also the one who has kicked the ball) run to put themselves behind their respective hurdle. At the same time the player in black runs to the ball: when he catches it he turns and shouts the name of the opponents who have not managed to put themselves in a prone position behind the hurdles. He scores a point for each name shouted.

All the players must carry out an overhead kick, one after the other.

Have as many goes as players and reverse the roles.

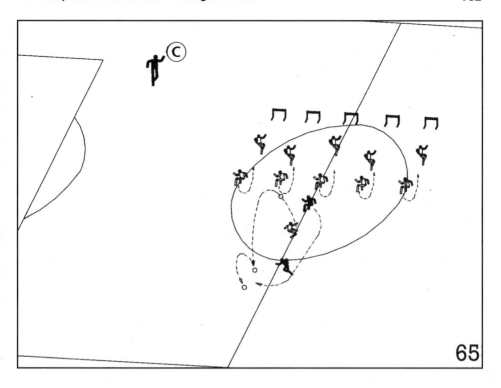

COACHING POINTS

As a variation, the player can carry out the overhead kick after the ball has been thrown to the ground by a teammate.

The breaks should be adapted to the age and characteristics of the players.

For the overhead kick, ask the players to kick the ball at chest height.

GAME 66

OBJECTIVE

- Speed/Endurance.
- Speed of performance.

Team game: played by 2 teams.
Playing area: a smaller field without goals, whose dimensions depend on the number of players.

While running, the players of a team pass one another the ball after dropping it from their hands and kicking it with the instep, or by drop-kick or header.

Each go is won by the team that carries out the higher number of passes in the pre-established time.

The game is won by the team that reaches the pre-established score first.

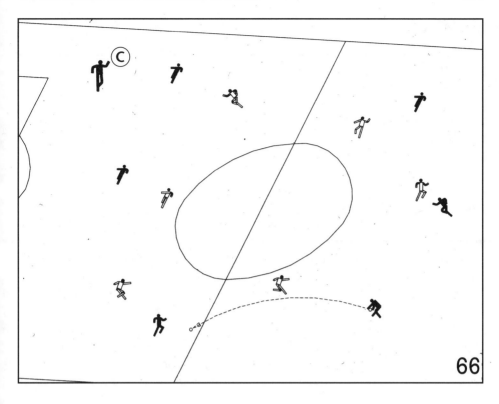

66

COACHING POINTS

Ask the players to watch the position of their teammates even when they are off the ball.

GAME 67

OBJECTIVE

- Speed/Endurance.
- Shots with the instep.
- Dribbling.

Individual game.

Place various objects (hurdles, fake walls for practicing free-kicks and cardboard boxes, all to be used as hiding places) at different distances (between 10 and 20 yards) from the midfield. The empty space of the hurdles should be covered with towels, playsuits or rags. Player A is in standing position at a distance of about 2 yards from a ball in the midfield. All the others sit in a line on the left and on the right of the ball, with their backs to the "hiding places". In turn, one of the sitting players stands up and kicks the ball with the instep: then he runs to hide behind one object, followed by the other players. Player A quickly runs to retrieve the ball and takes it back to its former position. Then he gets close to the hiding places to look for the hiding players and when he spots one he shouts his name (B) along with the position of the object he is hiding behind.

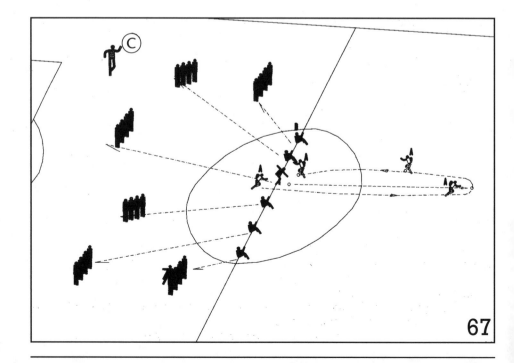

67

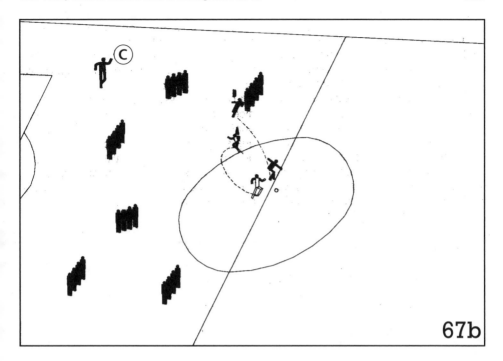

67b

At this moment players A and B run to the ball. If A is first on the ball, he touches it with the sole of his foot: B becomes his "prisoner" and sits in the midfield near the ball. Instead, if B is first on the ball he kicks it far with the instep and runs back to hide (along with the other "prisoners"); player A runs and retrieves the ball, takes it back to its former position and then he gets close to the hiding places. The coach calls out a third player, C, whom A still has not found out. If C is first on the ball he can kick the ball and thus set free his teammates sitting in the midfield who can hide again while A is retrieving the ball.

After a pre-established time, player A is replaced. Play one go per player.

At the end of each go the opponents sitting in the midfield ("prisoners") are counted: the winner is he who has captured the highest number of prisoners. When more players are captured they carry out an exercise while waiting to be set free.

COACHING POINTS

Breaks should be adapted to the players' age and characteristics.
Shots: the supporting foot is sideways to the ball and the last step is longer, with movement of the hip and of the knee of the kicking leg.

Kick the ball with the part of the foot just under the shoe-strings; the kicking leg follows the ball.

GAME 68

OBJECTIVE

- Juggling.
- Developing awareness and vision.

Team game: played by 2 teams.
Each team is arranged in a line, at a distance of 5-6 yards from each other; all the players and the coach have a ball.

The players must juggle the ball with the part of that body that the coach shows.

The coach starts the game by keeping the ball in front of the forehead, then in front of the chest, on the right thigh, on the left instep, on the outside of the right foot, on the instep and on the right thigh alternately, etc...

All the players must juggle the ball following his sequence: when the coach keeps the ball in front of his forehead the players can only juggle the ball with headers; when he keeps the ball on his right thigh they can only juggle the ball with the right thigh and so forth.

The juggling sequences follow one another with an irregular rhythm: each one should last about 5-10 seconds. In this way the players do not get used to carrying out the exercise with automatic rhythm.

When the coach gives the directions he should count the seconds of each performance to himself, while watching the two teams at the same time.

Without interrupting the game, the coach gives a point to the team whose players are quicker and more careful in passing to the next sequence.

The winner is the team that reaches the pre-established score first.

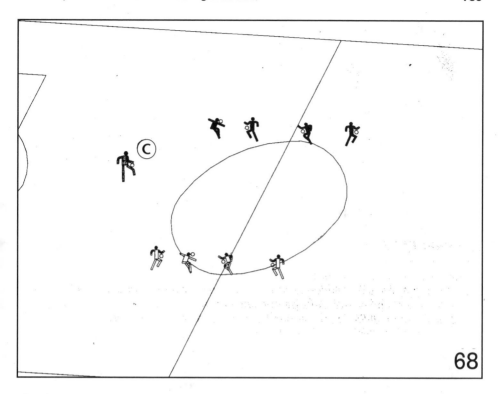

COACHING POINTS

Keep your feet outstretched and parallel to the ground; do not make the ball spin.

When juggling with headers, keep your body under the ball.

Ask the players to watch the beginning of the air phase of the ball, soon after the touch.

GAME 69

OBJECTIVE

• Juggling while moving.

Team game: played by 2 teams.
All the players are numbered. With some paint trace two 2-yard-wide and 10/15-yard-long parallel tracks on the ground. These tracks should be irregular: partly zigzagging, partly straight, partly wider and partly narrower. Each team places itself in front of a track: the players with the same number must be along the same line.

The coach calls out a number while all the players are carrying out a juggling exercise using the weakest part of the body. The players with that number immediately run to the track and try to reach the other end while juggling; when a player gets out of the track or when the ball bounces on the ground more than once he goes back to the starting point. The player who reaches the other end first or who is more advanced in the track after 15-20 seconds scores a point for his team.

Have as many goes as players.

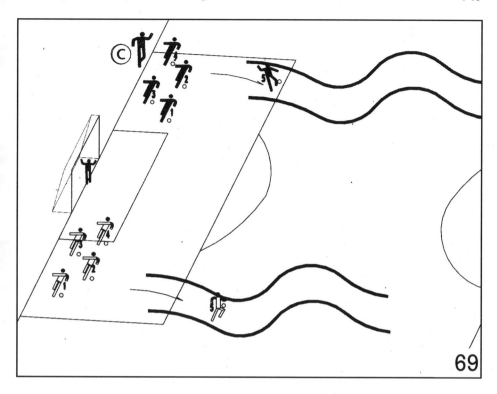

COACHING POINTS

Keep your feet outstretched and parallel to the ground; do not make the ball spin.

When juggling with headers keep your body under the ball.

GAME 70

OBJECTIVE

- Air control of the ball.
- Awareness.

Team game: played by 2 teams.

All the players are numbered and have a ball. With some paint, trace two 5/6-yard-wide and 10/15-yard-long straight tracks on the ground at a distance of 5-6 yards from each other. In the middle of each track form a line of 2-yard spaced flags from the beginning to the end. Each team places itself in front of a track and carries out the juggling sequence shown by the coach.

When the coach calls out a number, the players with that number run to the opposite end of their track: they make the ball bounce and kick it over the flags in a zigzagging way. The players kick the ball with the outstretched right instep to the left over the flags, then sprint through the flags to the left the ball so that after the bounce they can kick it again to the right over the flags with the outstretched left instep and so forth up to the end of the track. The most skilled players slalom through the flags without letting the ball touch the ground: they control it with the instep or the thigh and then kick it again, or they volley-juggle it while slaloming. The players must pay attention not to make the ball go out of the track and must watch the opponents as two or three of them change their places.

The first player to reach the end of the track scores a point; a point is also scored by the player who can say the names of the opponents who changed positions.

Have as many goes as players.

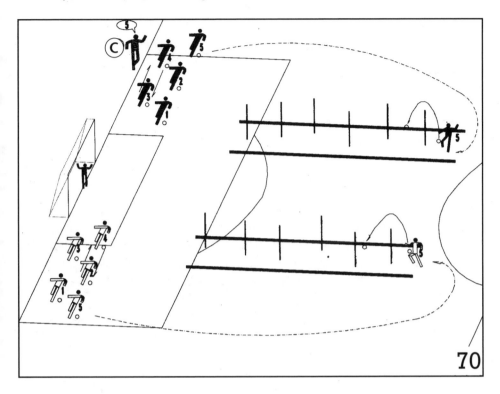

70

COACHING POINTS

The feet are outstretched and parallel to the ground.

  Ask the players to watch as soon as the air phase of the ball starts, that is immediately after the kick.

GAME 71

OBJECTIVE

- Air control.
- Endurance.
- Speed of performance.

Team game: played by 2 teams.

Scatter some objects here and there. Each team is divided in groups of three and each group has a ball. When the coach gives the signal, the players of each group start from the midfield and move forward up to the penalty area in a triangle-shaped arrangement while doing this exercise: one of them throws the ball upwards with his hands and, after a bounce or by volley, passes it to a teammate who passes it to the next teammate and so forth. If the pass is made after the second bounce the group goes back to the midfield and starts again.

Each group scores a point for its team when it reaches the penalty area, then quickly returns to the midfield to start the exercise again.

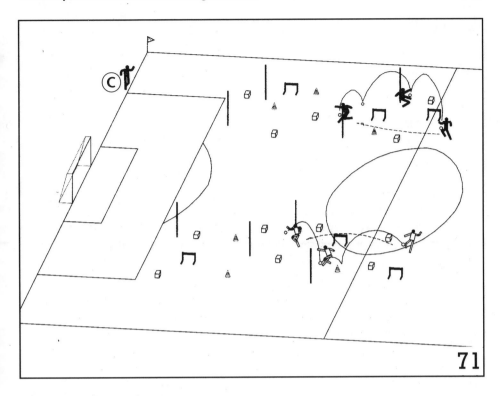

COACHING POINTS

Kick the ball with the outstretched foot.
Have suitable breaks.

GAME 72

OBJECTIVE

- Air control.
- Endurance.
- Speed of performance.

This game is a variation of game 71.
The playing area is reduced according to the number of players by two parallel lines of cones starting from the midfield up to the penalty area. The teams are divided in groups of three: the groups in black are arranged in the midfield and those in white in front of the penalty area.

When the coach gives the signal, each team's groups start the exercise: the groups in black must go forward up to the penalty area, those in white up to the midfield. The groups that let the ball bounce more than once are penalized: they must stop for 10 seconds.

The go is won by the team that takes all its players to the finishing line first.

The winner is the team that has won more goes at the end of the pre-established number of goes.

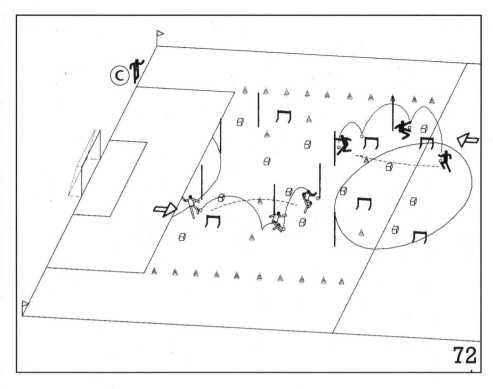

COACHING POINTS

Kick the ball with the outstretched foot.
Have suitable breaks.

GAME 73

OBJECTIVE

• Speed in controls and passes.

Team game: played by 2 teams.
The field is reduced according to the number of players. One or two players act as "extra" players and play with the team that wins the ball.
   The players of the two teams volley-pass the ball to each other. A team scores a point when its players manage to make four or five consecutive passes to each other without the opponents' touch or interception.
When a team scores a point or when the ball is touched by the opponents, the latter get possession of the ball.

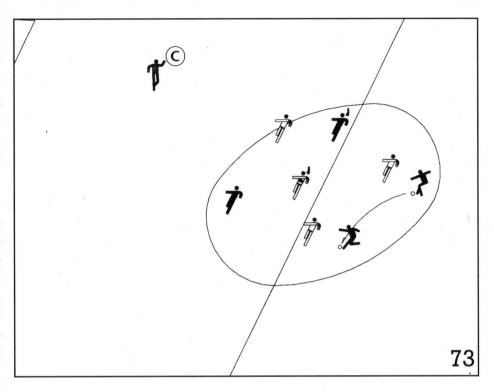

COACHING POINTS

Ask the players to watch even when they are off the ball.

GAME 74

OBJECTIVE

- Endurance/speed.
- Speed of performance.
- Long passes with the inside of the instep.
- Awareness

Team game: played by 2 teams.
The players are numbered and a circuit is made inside the penalty area. The team in black is arranged outside the penalty area near its top corner and carries out an exercise, either individually or in pairs. The players in white are arranged in the midfield circle.

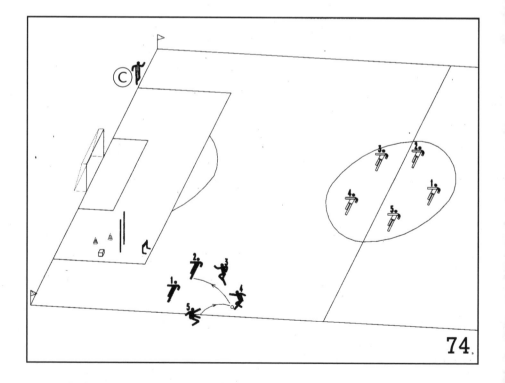

74.

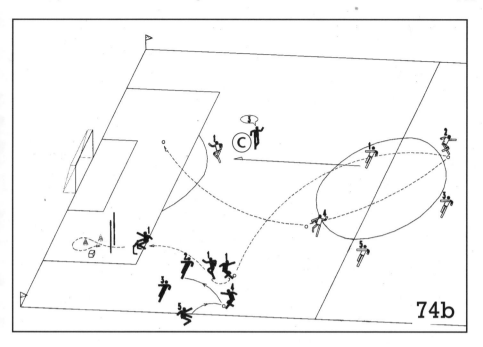

74b

When the coach gives the signal, player 1 in black kicks the ball to the midfield and immediately starts running forward in the circuit, then he runs back. Meanwhile, player 1 in white quickly reaches the penalty area and his teammates, after retrieving the ball and making two compulsory passes, pass it to him with a third pass into the penalty area.

At this moment, if the player in black has already finished the circuit he scores a point for his team; instead, if he is still running the point is scored by the team in white.

After players 1 have returned to their place players 2 carry out the exercise in the same way and so do the other players.

When all the players in black have run in the circuit the teams reverse their roles.

COACHING POINTS

Have suitable breaks.

Long passes: the run-up is diagonal to the direction of the shot; the hip and the knee of the kicking leg are slightly rotated outward.

The upper body is bent over the supporting leg and the ball is touched with the inside of the instep.

GAME 75

OBJECTIVE

- Accurate shots with the inside of the instep.

Individual game.

This game is played in groups and each player has more than one ball. The players of each group take turns to try to hit a target: this target can be either a ball or a pile of cones placed at a distance of 15-20 yards from the midfield line.

The first player shoots at the target: if he hits it he retrieves the ball, if he does not he leaves it near the target.

Then the second player shoots and so on.

The players who run out of balls are eliminated and make up a new group.

The winner is the last to run out of balls.

The game can also have a time limit: in this case the winner is the player with more balls at the end of the pre-established time.

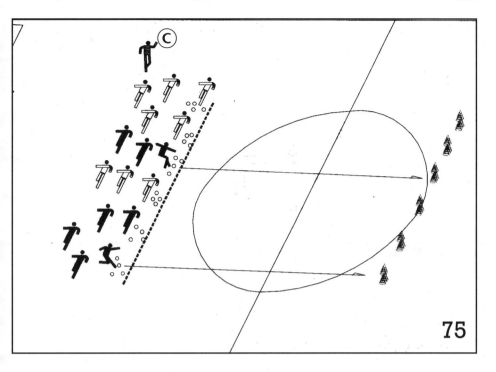

75

COACHING POINTS

When shooting with the instep the supporting foot is next to the ball with its tip pointing at the shooting direction; the last step is longer and the run-up is perpendicular to the ball.

The throw of the leg starts from the hip: the body is bent forward and the kicking leg follows the ball.

GAME 76

OBJECTIVE

- Air control follow-up.
- Juggling.
- Speed of performance.
- Endurance.

This game is in pairs.

The players are arranged in pairs as shown in the diagram; one player has his back to the goal, while the other is opposite him at a distance of 8-10 yards with a ball in his hands. When the coach gives the signal, the player with the ball throws it to his teammate with his hands; the latter moves to it, controls it without letting it touch the ground and then moves forward (still without letting it touch the ground) juggling it with any part of the body. If he fails to control the ball the pair goes a step back and starts again. If the juggling player drops the ball he must stop and wait for his teammate to throw him the ball again so that he can start the juggling exercise again. The pairs go to the midfield and the juggling player goes beyond the midfield line. When they have reached the midfield the pairs exchange their roles and start the same exercise up to the penalty area.

The pair who finishes the exercise first scores a point.

The winner is the pair with the higher score at the end of the pre-established number of goes, or that reaches the pre-established score first.

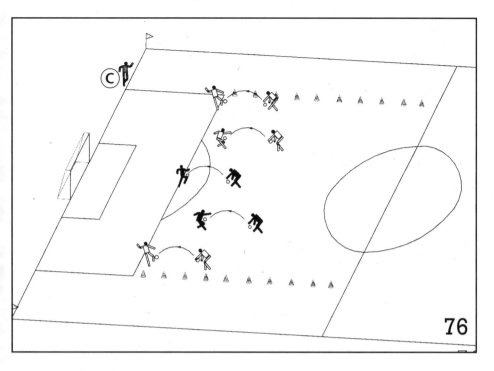

COACHING POINTS

Have suitable breaks.

When juggling, the instep is outstretched and parallel to the ground.

The coach moves with the players and gives advice on the control technique.

GAME 77

OBJECTIVE

- Ball control.
- Headers.
- Elevation.

Individual game.

This game is played in groups and each player has more than one ball. Each group plays on one side of a sort of net made up of two flags with a tape, or many flags along the same line. 3-4 yards from the net, on the other side, form a sort of circle with 15-20 balls at a distance of half a yard from one another.

In turns, starting from a distance of 3 yards from the net, each player drops a ball from his hands and, after a bounce, kicks it with the out-stretched instep (practice with both feet) and then heads it over the net down to the balls beyond: each ball hit and moved is won. If no ball is hit the ball is lost.

The winner is the player with more balls at the end of the pre-established time.

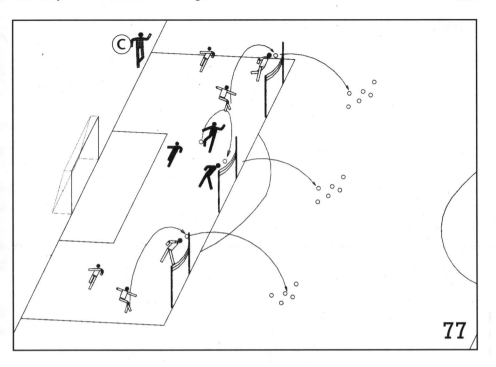

COACHING POINTS

When heading the ball, take-off on only one foot; the last step is longer and the ball must be hit with the center of the forehead.

GAME 78

OBJECTIVE

- Ball control with headers
- Speed/Endurance
- Coordination in pairs

Team game: played by 2 teams.
Playing area: the penalty area.
Set up two lines of obstacles (cones, hurdles, boxes, etc.) along the width of the penalty area. Two pairs, each with a ball, move along the lines while heading the ball back and forth. If the ball touches the ground, the pair must start again from the beginning.

The winner is the pair who takes the ball to the opposite side first.

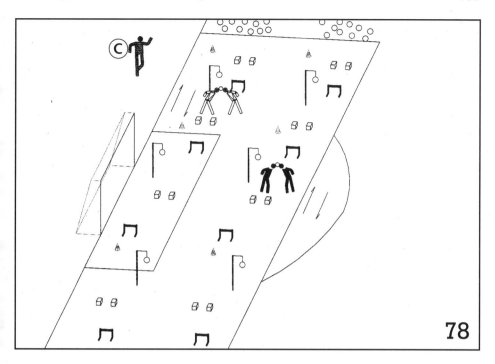

COACHING POINTS

The penalty for a dropped ball can be adjusted for skill level. For example, less skilled players need only go back to the last obstacle and continue from that point.

Have suitable breaks.

GAME 79

OBJECTIVE

- Ball control.
- Awareness.
- Speed/Endurance.
- Coordination in pairs.

This game is a variation of game 78.

Each pair has several balls and both players in a pair take one in one hand, while with the other they hold the end of a stick (thus being "tied" to each other). They drop the ball and juggle it forward after the bounce with the outstretched instep up to the opposite side. If the ball falls on the ground the pairs stops, picks it up and restarts juggling from the beginning. The winner is the pair who takes all the balls to the opposite side first.

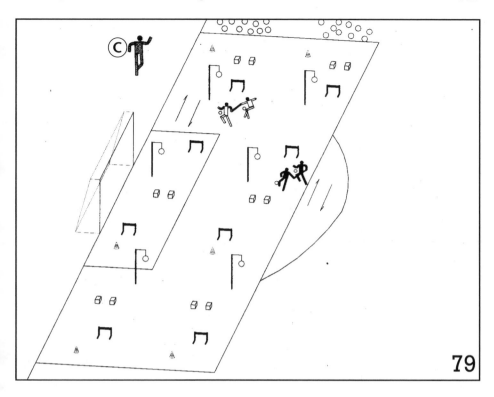

COACHING POINTS

The sequence of juggling should be determined according to the players' skills.
Have suitable breaks.

GAME 80

OBJECTIVE

- Speed/Endurance.
- Preliminary exercise to shots with the instep.

Team game: played by 2 teams.

The players in black are in a prone position on the midfield circle; inside the midfield circle there is a 3-4 yard cone-marked square with 3 or 4 balls inside. All the players in white are arranged around the circle of those in black, except three: one of them is inside the cone-marked square with a ball in his hand, the two others are inside the circle made up of the players in black.

When the coach gives the signal the first player of the team in black quickly gets up and runs along the midfield circle, jumping over his teammates. At the same time the player in white inside the square drops the ball and shoots at the running opponent. He scores a point every time he hits him.

Meanwhile the players in white outside the midfield circle retrieve the balls and pass them to the two teammates inside, who run to the square where they place the balls. All this goes on till the running player in black gets back to his former sitting position. Then the second player in black quickly gets up, runs along the midfield circle jumping over his teammates until he gets back to his former sitting position, while the players in white carry out the same exercise as before. When all the players in black have run along the midfield circle the roles are reversed.

Have as many goes as players, so that in turn everybody can play inside the square.

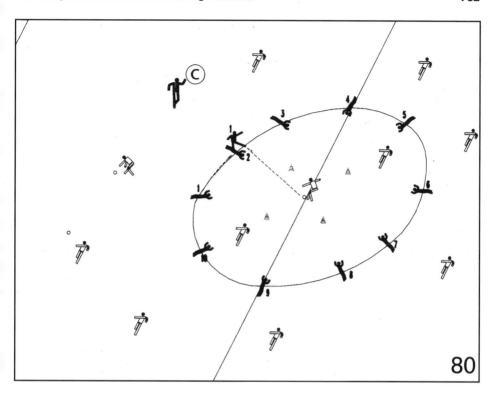

80

COACHING POINTS

Shots with the instep: the ball must be kicked with the part of the foot under the shoe-strings; the kicking leg follows the ball.

GAME 81

OBJECTIVE

- Speed of performance.
- Speed/Endurance.
- Preliminary exercise to shots with the instep.

This game is a variation of game 80.
The players in black are numbered and in a sitting position on the midfield circle. Every 5-10 seconds the coach calls out the numbers, thus giving the player inside the square more targets and more tension.

The player inside the square cannot get out and shoots, dropping the ball from his hands.

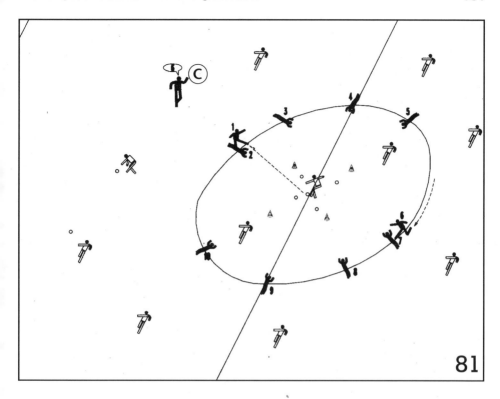

81

COACHING POINTS

Have suitable breaks when calling the players.
Shots with the instep: the ball must be kicked with the part of the foot under the shoe-strings; the kicking leg follows the ball.

GAME 82

OBJECTIVE

- Shooting with the instep.

Individual game.

The game is played with groups of 5-6 players. For each group place 10-15 flags in such a way as to form two parallel lines which should be 2-3 yards from each other.

Each player has 5-6 balls and takes a turn shooting them with the instep from a distance of 15 yards from the flags: the ball must travel along the corridor formed by the flags.

If the ball touches the flags or gets out of the corridor the player must retrieve it; instead, if the ball reaches the end of the corridor it must be left where it is.

The winner of the go is the player who finishes his balls first.

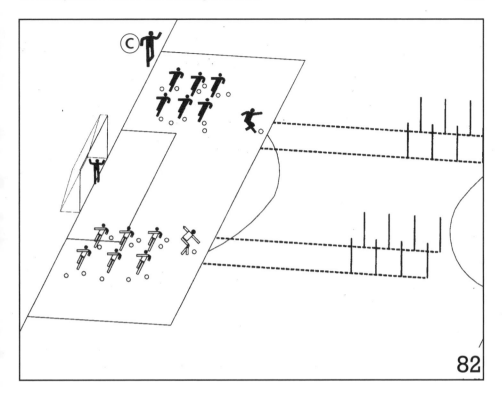

COACHING POINTS

Shots with the instep:
- the supporting foot is sideways to the ball, the last step is longer and the movement must start from the hip;
- the knee of the kicking leg is bent over the ball;
- the ball must be kicked with the part of the foot just under the shoe-strings; the kicking leg follows the ball, while the upper body is bent forward.

GAME 83

OBJECTIVE

- Shots with the instep making the ball spin.

This game is a variation of game 82.
Form a 15-yard-long funnel-shaped corridor for each group by using flags: it should be 3 yards wide at the beginning. With some cones, form a 5-6 yard square on the right and on the left of each corridor. In turns, one player kicks the ball, then runs after it and shoots it again with the inside of the foot. The ball must travel close to the flags and end in the cone-marked square. If a player sends the ball outside the square he retrieves it. Practice both the right and the left foot.

The winner of the go is the player who finishes his balls first.

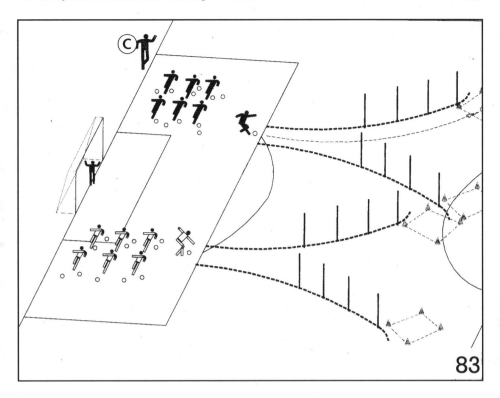

83

COACHING POINTS

The corridor helps the player: widen or narrow it according to skill level.

Shots with the inside of the instep:
- the run-up must make a 45 degree angle with regard to the direction of the shot;
- the supporting foot is slightly behind and sideways to the ball;
- rotate the hip and the knee outward;
- the tip of the kicking foot is slightly raised;
- the ball must be kicked below the middle and with the inside of the big toe, then of the foot;
- the kicking leg follows the ball while the supporting leg carries out a small leap forward.

GAME 84

OBJECTIVE

- Individual work.
- Control of the ball.

This game is played by 2 or more teams.

The teams are arranged by each other's side, with the players forming a line behind 3-4 hurdles.

At the end of the hurdles, on the right, there is a cone-marked 4 yard square.

More forward, at a distance if about 6 yards from the square, there is a teammate with a ball.

When the coach gives the signal the player with the ball throws it upward above the square with his hands: at the same time the first player of the line quickly slaloms through the hurdles, runs to the square, controls the ball with his chest, thigh or foot and then passes it back to his teammate. He must control the ball and pass it back after only one bounce or without letting it touch the ground at all: if he fails he goes to the back of the line and does the exercise again, if he succeeds then he carries out an individual ball control exercise while waiting for his teammates to finish. He throws the ball upward and forward, controlling it with his chest, thigh and instep alternately. The same exercise is carried out by each player who has finished.

After each repetition the player at the end of the circuit with the hurdles is replaced and the team moves to the left of the square.

The go is won by the team that is the first to go to the individual work with all its players.

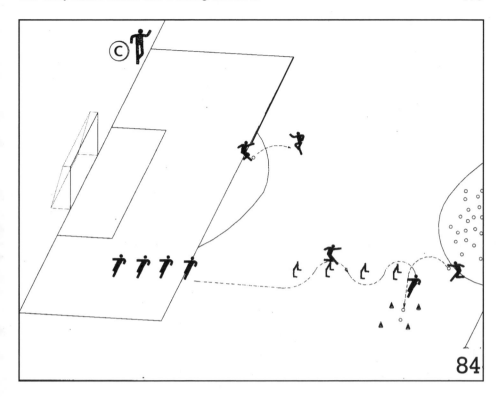

84

COACHING POINTS

In the individual work, coach ball control also with moving pairs.
When controlling the ball, the part of the body involved should not be stiff: the ball must touch a part that is already moving in its same direction.

GAME 85

OBJECTIVE

- Speed of performance - Endurance.
- Wall pass.
- Preliminary exercise to diving headers.

This game is played by 2 or more teams.
Place two lines of cones parallel to the sidelines on the wings.

The teams are arranged side by side, with the players divided in pairs and forming a line.

Each team has two balls placed in front of the pairs, at a distance of 1-2 yards and 20-25 yards respectively.

When the coach gives the signal, the players of each team's first pair run forward and wall-pass the ball to each other up to the second ball. When they reach the second ball they leave the first one and take back the second with different passes. One of the two players puts himself in the prone position next to the first cone: from a distance of 5-6 yards, the other throws him a high ball some yards forward with his hands. His teammate immediately gets up, runs to the ball, passes it back with a header (if he fails with the header the pair takes two steps back) and then lies down in the prone position next to the second cone. In this way the two players go back to the starting point.

When the first pair has finished the exercise the second one starts.

The go is won by the team that finishes the pair work first. After each repetition, the roles in the pairs are reversed.

The winner is the team that reaches the pre-established score first.

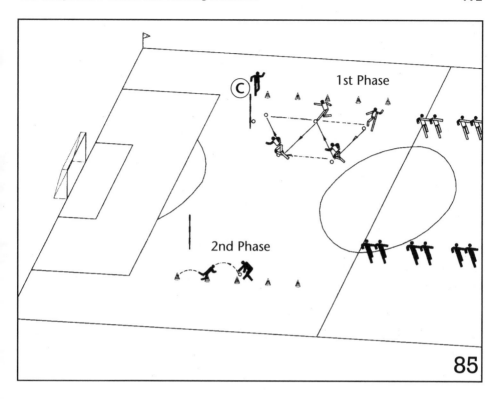

COACHING POINTS

Passes: the supporting foot is slightly behind the ball.
Headers: hit the ball with the center of the forehead.
Prone position: the elbows form a 90 degree angle and are higher than the shoulders. When switching to the upright position push hard on the arms.

GAME 86

OBJECTIVE

- Shots with the instep.
- Speed of performance - Sudden sprint.
- Ability to consider distances according to one's own skills.

This game is played by 2 or more 6-7 player teams.

The teams are arranged by each other's side on the midfield line.

When the coach gives the signal the first player of each team drops the ball from his hands and after a bounce he kicks it upward and forward with the instep to a distance of 3-4 yards; then he runs to the ball, catches it and stops. The second player starts from where the first player stopped: he drops the ball, kicks it after the bounce, runs and catches it, then stops. The third player starts from where the second player has stopped and so forth. After the last player has done the exercise the first one starts again and the exercise goes on as described until the players reach the goal line. If a player fails to catch the ball before it touches the ground he takes three steps back and his team is penalized: it stops for 5 seconds.

The winner is the team whose player reaches the goal line first.

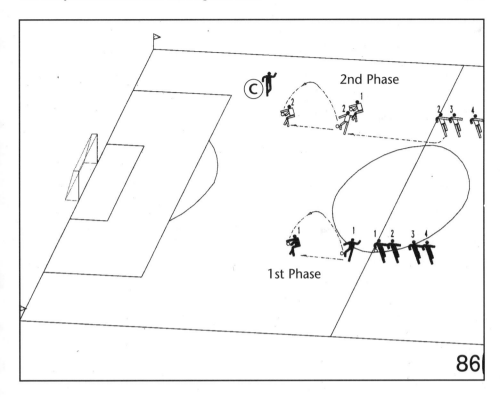

2nd Phase

1st Phase

86

COACHING POINTS

Kick the ball with the part of the foot under the shoe-strings; the foot is outstretched and parallel to the ground.

GAME 87

OBJECTIVE

- Stopping the ball.
- Speed of performance.
- Sudden sprint.
- Ability to consider distances according to one's own skills.

This game is a variation of game 86.
Instead of catching the ball the players stop it with the thigh or the instep or under the sole of the foot.

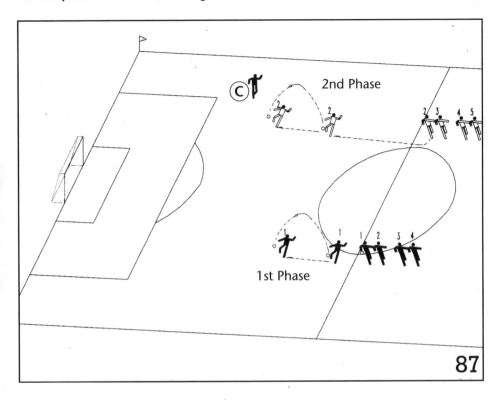

COACHING POINTS

The part of the body that stops the ball must not be stiff: it moves backward one moment before touching the ball, and the ball meets a part that moves in the same direction.

GAME 88

OBJECTIVE

- Juggling.
- Headers.
- Sudden sprints.

This game is played by 2 or more 6-8 player teams.
The teams each have a ball and are arranged near the goal line.

When the coach gives the signal the first player of each team drops the ball from his hands and, after the bounce, kicks it with the outstretched foot: then he heads it, trying to send it as far as possible to the opposite goal line and stops. The second player starts and reaches the ball: he does exactly the same thing as his teammate, and so do the next players. After the last player the first one starts again.

The game goes on like this until the ball reaches the opposite goal line. A point is scored by the team that reaches the goal line first; then the exercise is performed in the opposite direction.

The team that reaches the pre-established score first is the winner.

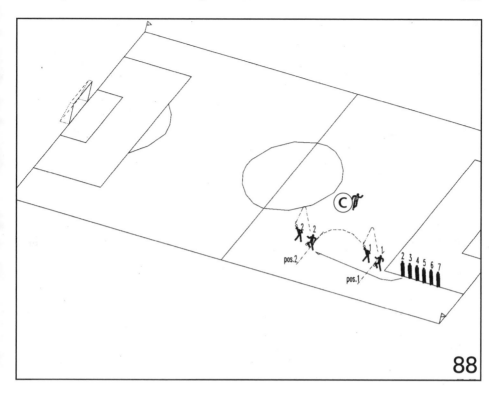

COACHING POINTS

Juggling: the foot is outstretched and parallel to the ground.
Headers: the ball must be hit with the center of the forehead.
The feet are one in front of the other: before heading the ball the weight of the body shifts from the leg behind to the leg forward.

GAME 89

OBJECTIVE

- Juggling.

Individual game.
Each player has a ball and stands in a line on the midfield line.

When the coach gives the signal, the players carry out a ball juggling sequence. They kick the ball up by alternating their feet and let it bounce once. At a certain moment the coach stops the exercise and watches the players' position with regard to their starting point. The player closer to the starting line scores a point; then all the players go back to the starting line to start again.

The winner is the player to reach the pre-established score first.

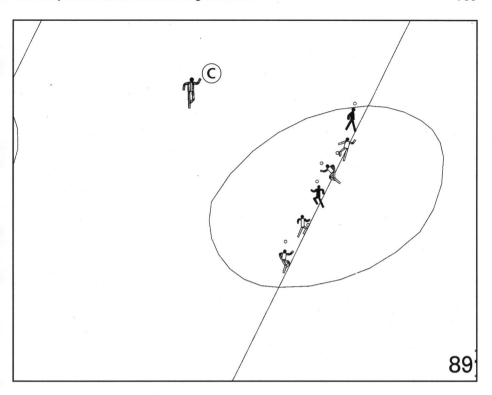

COACHING POINTS

When juggling, the foot is outstretched and parallel to the ground; the ball is kicked with the part of the foot under the shoe-strings.

GAME 90

OBJECTIVE

- Speed.
- Speed of performance.
- Stopping the ball and turning around.

This game is played by 2 or more 6-8 player teams.
Each team is arranged before the midfield line with lots of balls nearby. In front of each team place a line of 5-6 yard-spaced cones.

When the coach gives the signal, the first two players (A and B) of each team start, while the others carry out individual or pair work on ball control. Player A stops near the first cone with a ball in his hands; player B runs after him, then goes beyond him and stops near the second cone where he receives and controls the ball passed to him by A. B stops the ball and turns around to the third cone, where meanwhile A has reached in order to receive the ball that is going to be passed to him by B, who will then reach the fourth cone: the exercise goes on like this, with the two players alternating at passing and controlling the ball cone after cone. When the two players have reached the last cone they leave the ball there and quickly run back to the starting point where they practice ball control with one of the other balls. At the same time the next two players start and carry out the same exercise.

A point is scored by the team that takes all its balls to the end of the cones first.

The game is won by the team that reaches the pre-established score first.

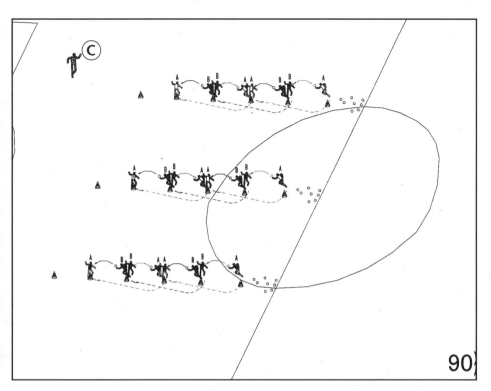

90

COACHING POINTS

- Stopping the ball with the legs and turning around: the part of the body that controls the ball must be relaxed. When controlling with the thigh, it moves backward and downward one moment before touching the ball. At the same time the supporting foot slightly leaps and acts as a pivot.
- Stopping the ball with the chest and turning around: the feet are one in front of the other and there is a slight leap on both of them while a rotation of the upper body is carried out. Thanks to the slight leap, the body can turn to the desired direction and the ball can be controlled better.

GAME 91

OBJECTIVE

- Quickness of reflexes.
- Speed of performance.
- Sudden sprint.

This game can be played by two or more teams.

Playing area: a 20 x 10 yard cone-marked rectangle similar to a volleyball court, divided in two halves either with two flags and a tape or with a thick line of flags.

Each team is made up of three or four players. Two teams play with a ball in each playing area.

The players of a team are arranged in a line at the end of their side: the rules are those of table-tennis doubles. The first player of a team serves with any part of the body except the hands and sends the ball over the tape to the opposing side, then he quickly goes to the back of the line.

The first player of the opposing team shoots back, either by volleying the ball or kicking it after a bounce, then goes to the back of his line.

The first player of the other team shoots back and then goes to the back of the line and so forth. Of course each player tries to send the ball in the most difficult place for the opponents to reach.

A point is scored when the ball bounces more than once in the opposing field, when the opponents send the ball out, or when they touch it with their hands. The winner is the team that reaches the pre-established score first.

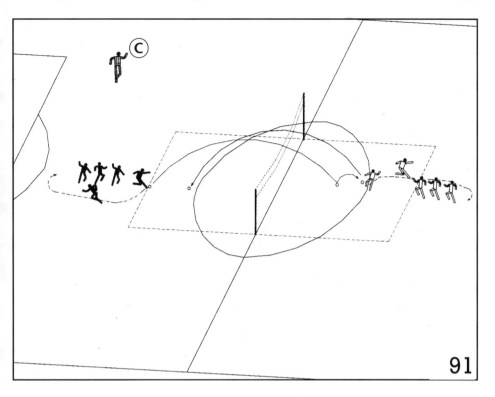

91

COACHING POINTS

Practice with both feet.

GAME 92

OBJECTIVE

- Speed of performance.
- Speed/Endurance.

Team game: played by 2 teams.
The game is played in a smaller field, without goals.
  The players of a team pass the ball to each other as in a regular match.
  The team that carries out three consecutive volley-passes scores a point.
  The winner is the team that reaches the pre-established score first.

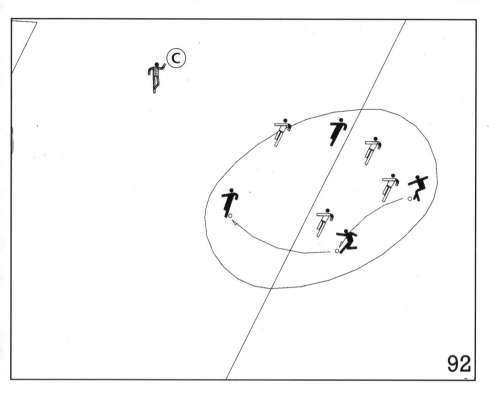

COACHING POINTS

Ask the players to watch the position of their teammates also when they are off the ball.

GAME 93

OBJECTIVE

- Juggling.
- Ball control.

Team game: played by 2 teams.
All the players have a ball.

By using cones, flags, chairs and bags, form a circular playing area inside the midfield circle, whose dimensions vary according to the number of players.

The two teams are arranged opposite each other on their respective sides.

When the coach gives the signal, all the players start juggling here and there, also after a bounce, one foot at a time. They should kick the ball after each step. As they move around, the coach shifts the objects, limiting the playing area by making it smaller.

A point is scored when an opponent sends the ball out or is caught juggling without moving around.

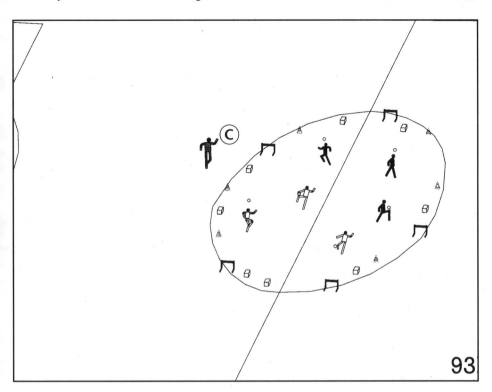

93

COACHING POINTS

The juggling foot is outstretched and parallel to the ground.
  The ball is kicked with upper part of the foot and the leg follows the ball up to waist-height.

GAME 94

OBJECTIVE

- Speed of performance.
- Shots with the inside of the foot.

Team game: played by 2 teams.

Playing area: make a circle inside the midfield circle by using flags at a distance of 3-4 yards from one another. Inside the circle formed by the flags and inside the ring that has been formed between the flags and the midfield circle, place an equal number of balls. The team in white plays in the ring and the one in black in the inner circle.

When the coach gives the signal, the players of each team kick the balls out of their field through the flags into the opposing one. When the coach whistles, the game stops and a point is scored by the team with fewer balls in its field.

After each repetition the teams change fields. If a player shoots the ball out of the midfield circle he quickly retrieves it.

The winner is the team to reach the pre-established score first.

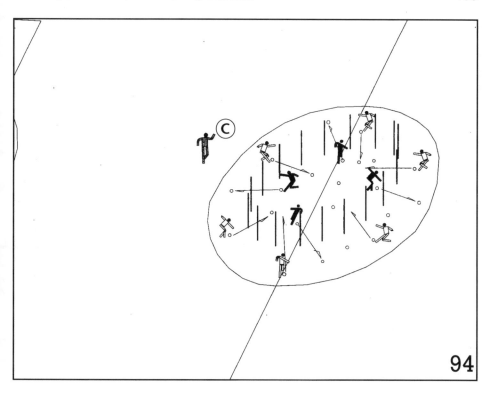

94

COACHING POINTS

Shots with the inside of the foot:
- the supporting foot is sideways to the ball, with the tip pointing towards the target;
- the kicking foot makes a 90 degree angle with regard to the supporting foot;
- the ball is kicked with the inside of the foot;
- the ball is kicked in the middle; the kicking leg makes a slightly backward and then forward movement, starting from the hip.

GAME 95

OBJECTIVE

- Speed of performance.
- Sudden sprint.
- Lobs.

Team game: played by 2 teams.
Each team has a ball. The teams are arranged in a row and are sitting opposite each other at a distance of 25-30 yards with a goal behind. Halfway between the two teams, two balls are placed along the same line, 6-7 yards from each other. After deciding which team each ball belongs to, the coach gives the starting signal.

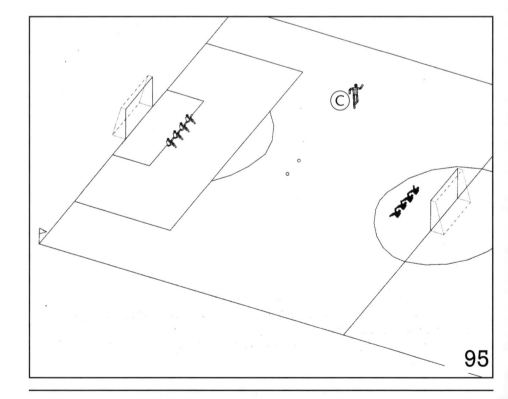

95

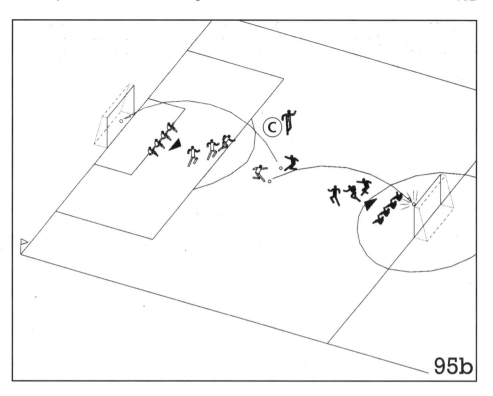

95b

The first player of each team runs to his team's ball and shoots it with the inside of the instep trying to score into the goal behind his opponents. When he is halfway on his run the coach gives a second signal and the other players from both teams quickly run to the ball to act as an obstacle. Each goal scores a point.

After putting the balls back to their place the same exercise is done by the second player of each team, then by the third and so on.

The winner is the team that reaches the pre-established score first.

COACHING POINTS

Shoots with the inside of the instep:
- the run-up makes a 45 degree angle with regard to the direction of the shot;
- slightly rotate the hip and the knee of the kicking leg outward;
- the upper body is tilted over the supporting leg;
- the ball must be kicked with the inside of the instep, with the toes slightly raised.

GAME 96

OBJECTIVE

- Quickness of reflexes.
- Spin shots.

This game can be played by two or more 4-5 player teams, or by two players on a smaller field.

Playing area: form a cone-marked 7-8 yard long and 15-20 yard wide rectangle. One of the long sides must be next to a high wall, at a distance of 5-6 yards from it.

A group of players is arranged in each side.

When the coach gives the signal the players send the ball to the wall by using any part of their body except their hands, so as to make the ball bounce into the opposing field; the opponents send the ball back in the same way. In this "clearing" game the ball can be volleyed or kicked after it has bounced once on the ground.

A point is scored when the opponents let the ball bounce on the ground more than once or if the ball kicked by the opponents goes out after it has bounced on the wall.

The winner is the team that reaches the pre-established score first.

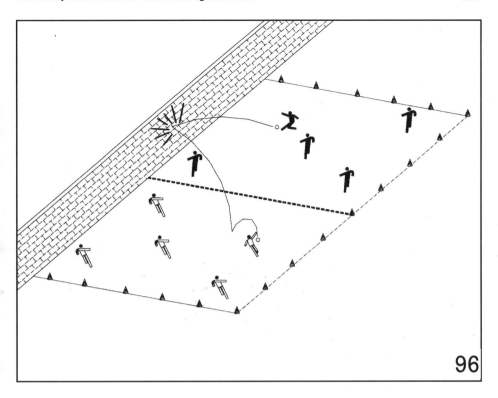

96

COACHING POINTS

The ball must be kicked under the middle: the supporting foot is slightly behind the ball and the tip of the kicking foot is slightly uplifted.

GAME 97

OBJECTIVE

- Sudden sprint.
- Quickness of reflexes.
- Spin shots.

This game is a variation of game 96.
The field is smaller, according to the number of players. The players of each group are arranged in a line behind a cone at the end of the field. The first player of each line shoots the ball to the wall trying to make the ball bounce and fall into the opposing field; the first opponent shoots the ball back in the same way, then the two players go to the back of the line. Then the second player of each team shoots in the same way and so forth. The game goes on like this for all the players, who take turns shooting the ball back.

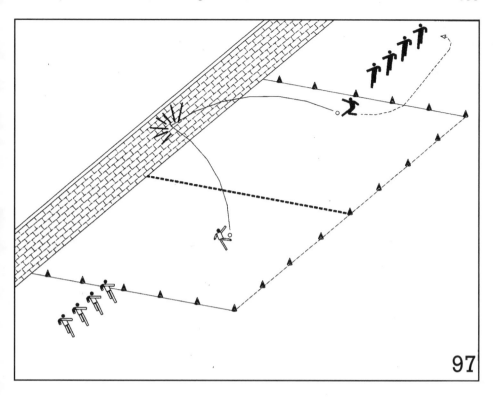

97

COACHING POINTS

Kick the ball under the middle; the tip of the kicking foot is slightly raised.
The supporting foot is slightly behind and sideways to the ball.

GAME 98

OBJECTIVE

- Accurate passes with the inside of the foot or with the instep.

This game can be played by 2 teams or by several 3-4 player groups.
Playing area: the midfield circle.

The team in black is arranged inside the midfield circle in open order while the players in white are arranged just outside it with three or four balls.

When the coach gives the signal, the players in white volley-pass the balls to one another making them pass across the field of the players in black who try to intercept them. A point is scored when a ball is intercepted.

The go has a time limit: after the pre-established time the teams change roles.

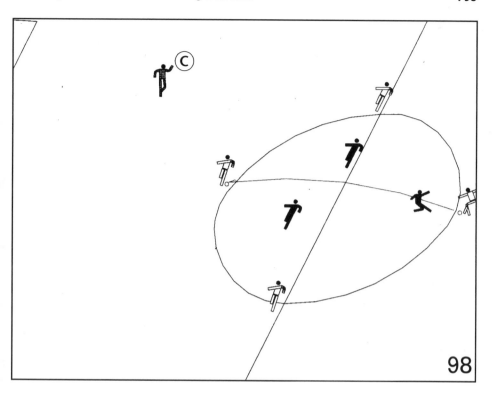

98

COACHING POINTS

Long passes with the instep:
- the supporting foot is next to the ball with the tip pointing towards the target;
- the tip of kicking foot is turned to the ground and the ankle is blocked;
- kick the ball in the middle;
- the kicking leg starts the movement from the hip, then the bent knee lowers on the ball and stretches to shoot and follow the ball.

GAME 99

OBJECTIVE

- Quickness of reflexes.
- Headers.
- Passes with spin shots.

Team game: played by 2 teams.

Playing area: the penalty area or the six yard area, according to the number of players. Trace the diagonals of the playing area by using cones. Place two thick lines of flags in the center, forming a sort of cross.

Each team is divided in two groups which are arranged in the opposite spaces obtained by tracing the diagonals.

When the coach gives the signal, after three passes the group in black must pass the ball to the teammates over the flags. The opponents score a point when they intercept the ball. After a pre-established time the teams' roles are reversed. The winner is the team to reach the pre-established score first.

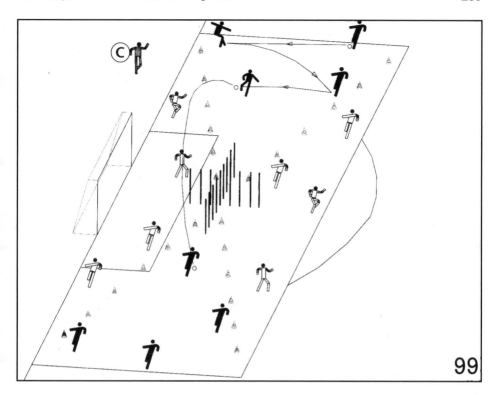

99

COACHING POINTS

Headers: hit the ball with the center of the forehead.
Spin pass: hit the ball below the middle with the inside of the big toe and with the tip of the foot slightly raised.
The supporting foot is slightly behind and sideways to the ball.

GAME 100

OBJECTIVE

- Quickness of reflexes.
- Headers.

Playing area: the penalty area or the six yard area, according to the number of players. Place a lot of flags on one diagonal of the rectangle of play (or place two flags on two opposite corners, then tie them with a tape) so as to divide the playing area in two triangles. In the two corners without flags mark two areas by using cones and place there a goalkeeper per each team.

The two teams are arranged on the two triangles marked by the diagonal, with the opposing goalkeeper in the area behind them as shown in the diagram.

When the coach gives the signal, after three passes the players try to send the ball to their goalkeeper (who is in the opposing field) by header over the flags. The opponents try to intercept the pass without entering the goalkeeper's area.

A point is scored when a player manages to pass the ball to his goalkeeper.

The winner is the team to reach the pre-established score first.

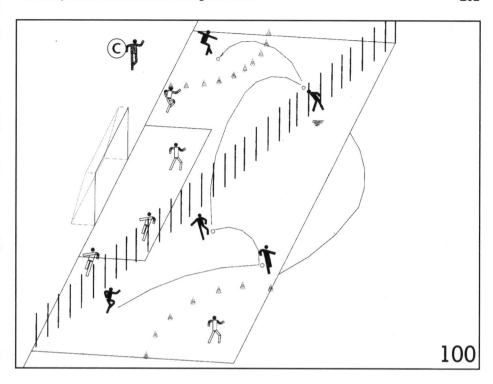

100

COACHING POINTS

Headers: hit the ball with the center of the forehead

GAME 101

OBJECTIVE

- Sudden sprint.
- Continuity of performance speed.
- Concentration.

Team game: played by 2 teams.
Playing area: place a thick line of flags along the edge of the six yard area. The players in black are sitting in a line near the flags or are divided in two groups and sitting on the sides of the six yard area. The team in white is arranged in a line outside the six yard area in front of the flags. Two coaches, C1 and C2, are at the corners of the penalty area. C1 is on the left of the flags and C2 on the right, they have several balls.

One player in white is in front of his teammates and has several balls which he must toss to them.

He throws the ball with his hands to the first teammate of the line, who heads it over the flags trying to score a goal; at the same time C1 shoots a ball into the six yard area.

The first player in black immediately stands up: he runs to the ball crossed by C1, settles it and clears it over the flags to the area of the team in white. Then he tries to also clear the ball headed by the first player in white: whether he succeeds or fails, he goes back to his former sitting position and C2 shoots a ball into the six yard area. The second player in black stands up and clears it: at the same time the player in white throws the ball to the second player of the line, who heads it over the flags trying to score a goal; the player in black must try to clear this ball too. The exercise goes on like this until the two coaches finish the balls.

After a certain number of balls the player in white who throws the balls to his teammates is replaced and the players in black who clear the balls change sides with the other group. At the end of each go the teams' roles are reversed: the players in black head the ball trying to score a goal, those in white clear the balls.

The winner is the team that has scored more goals after the pre-established number of goes.

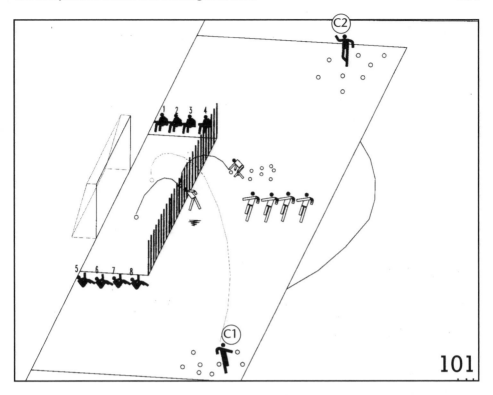

101

COACHING POINTS

Headers: hit the ball with the left, right or center of the forehead.
Take-off on only one foot; the last step is longer.

GAME 102

OBJECTIVE

- Sudden sprint.
- Continuity of performance speed.
- Concentration.
- Shots with the instep.

Team game: played by 2 teams.
Place three cone-marked 2.5 yard wide goals in the penalty area, at a distance of 6-7 yards from each other.

When the coach gives the signal, the players in white shoot from a distance of 5-6 yards outside the penalty area after receiving a pass from their teammate.

At the same time, in turns one player in black stands up and tries to prevent the ball from entering any goal.

After all the players in white have shot at goal the roles of the two teams are reversed.

Each goal scores a point.

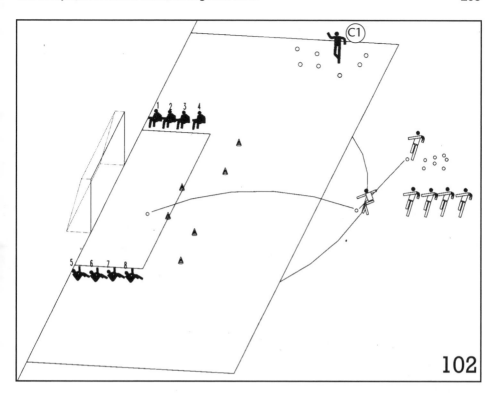

102

COACHING POINTS

Shots: the supporting foot is sideways and next to the ball, with the tip pointing towards the target.

The last step is longer; the tip of the kicking foot is turned to the ground and the ankle is blocked.

  Kick the ball in the middle.

  The supporting leg slightly bends one moment before the shot.

  The kicking leg starts the movement from the hip, then the bent knee lowers on the ball and stretches to shoot.

GAME 103

OBJECTIVE

- Deep passes at the right moment.
- Sprint, speed of performance.
- Concentration.
- Endurance.

Team game: played by 2 teams.

Playing area: with two lines of cones parallel to the midfield line mark a field whose dimensions vary according to the number of players.

The two lines are made up of 4 cones each arranged in such a way as to form two small goals on each side, as shown in the diagram.

The two teams are arranged in the field and one player per team is placed behind the opponents. The coach has a supply of balls and is placed just outside the field: he gives the starting signal by throwing a ball into the playing area.

The players of each team try to make a deep pass to their teammate behind the opponents. If they succeed, then the player dribbles the ball into one of the two small goals and quickly goes back to his starting position.

Exactly when one of the two teams carries out the deep pass the coach immediately throws a second ball into the playing area and the exercise continues in the same way. The game goes on until the coach runs out of balls.

The go is won by the team that takes more balls into the small goals.

At the end of each go the players who receive the deep pass are replaced.

Have as many goes as players.

The winner is the team that wins more goes.

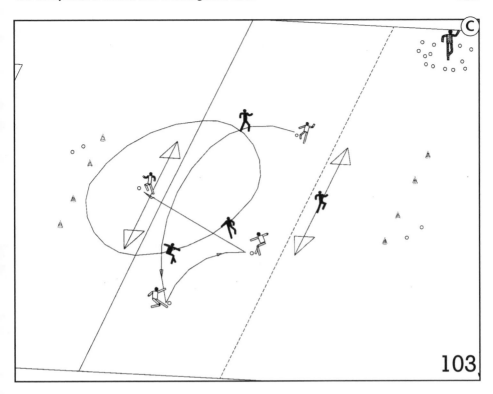

103

COACHING POINTS

The coach immediately throws the ball into the playing area so that the game is not interrupted.

Ask the players to carry out deep passes with low-ground shots with the instep or the inside of the foot.

The players must carry out the deep pass once their teammate has returned to the starting point after dribbling into the goal.

GAME 104

OBJECTIVE

- Deep penetrating passes at the right moment.
- Sprints, speed of performance.
- Concentration.
- Endurance.

This game is a variation of game 103.

By using cones, form corridors parallel to the midfield line and place one player of a different team into each of them, as shown in the diagram.

This player acts as a defender: without getting out of his corridor he must try to intercept the balls passed to his opponent. He moves sideways, following the direction of the ball and the position of the opponent behind him.

The same rules as those of **GAME 103** apply.

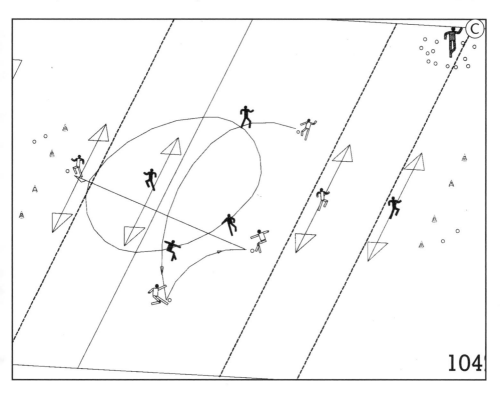

104

COACHING POINTS

The coach immediately throws the ball into the playing area so that the game is not interrupted.

Ask the players to carry out deep passes with low-ground shots with the instep or the inside of the foot.

The players must carry out the deep pass once their teammate has returned to the starting point after dribbling into the goal.

GAME 105

OBJECTIVE

- One-two passes.
- Sprints.
- Speed of action.
- Concentration.
- Endurance.

This game is a variation of game 104.
The attacker dribbles the ball into the small goal after a one-two pass with the teammate from whom he has received the ball.

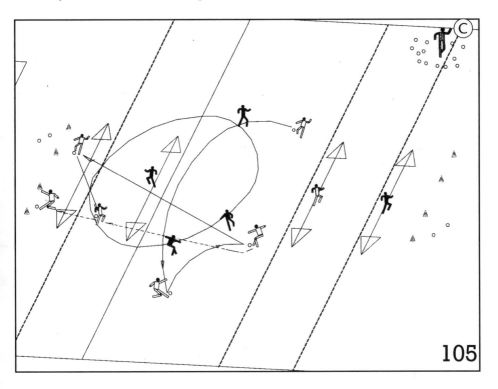

105

COACHING POINTS

The coach immediately throws the ball into the playing area so that the game is not interrupted.

The players must carry out the deep pass once their teammate has returned to the starting point after dribbling into the goal.

GAME 106

OBJECTIVE

- Deep penetrating passes.
- One-two passes.
- Speed of action.
- Concentration.
- Endurance.

Team game: played by 2 teams.

The playing area can be reduced according to the number of players. As shown in the diagram, form a 20-25 yard long cone-marked corridor stretching from one sideline to the other, at the end of which three small goals are placed. The teams are arranged in the central part except for three players per team: one plays as a defender in the part of the corridor belonging to his team, the other two play as attackers in the opponents' part of the corridor

The coach has a supply of balls and is placed outside the playing area.

The coach gives the starting signal by throwing a ball into the central part where the players try to win possession: they must make a deep pass to their teammates in the opponents' part of the corridor. When the ball reaches the opponents' corridor the three players play two on one. In order to score a point the attackers must win the ball, pass it to each other and dribble it into one of the three small goals without interception or touch by the defender.

If the defender touches the ball it is put back into the coach's supply of balls.

Exactly when one of the two teams passes the ball to the corridor the coach immediately throws a second ball into the central part and the players continue the exercise without interruptions. The game goes on until the coach runs out of balls.

The go is won by the team that takes more balls into the small goals.

At the end of each go the players who receive the deep pass are replaced.

The winner is the team that reaches the pre-established score first.

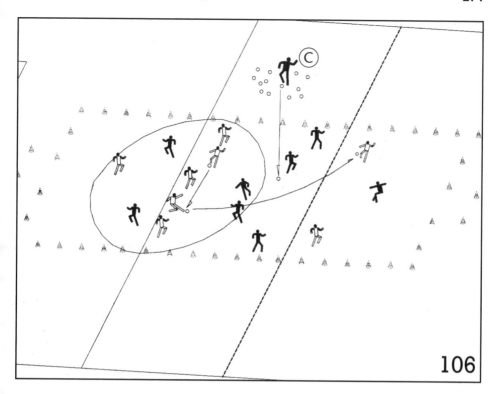

106

COACHING POINTS

The coach immediately throws the ball into the playing area so that the game is not interrupted.

The players must carry out the deep pass once their teammate has returned to the starting point after dribbling into the goal.

GAME 107

OBJECTIVE

- Deep penetrating passes.
- Speed of performance.
- Concentration.
- Endurance.

Team game: played by 2 teams.

According to the number of players, the playing area is reduced by two lines of cones perpendicular to the goal line. At a distance of 10 yards from each end of the field place three 3-yard-wide cone-marked small goals. No defender can enter the penalty area.

The coach has several balls and is placed near a sideline of the playing area.

The teams play as in a regular match on the smaller field: a goal is valid only when a player dribbles the ball into one of the small goals after a deep pass from a teammate. The former can enter the penalty area only when the ball enters it too. Exactly when the ball enters the penalty area the coach immediately throws a second ball into the field and the players continue the exercise without interruptions. The game goes on until the coach runs out of balls.

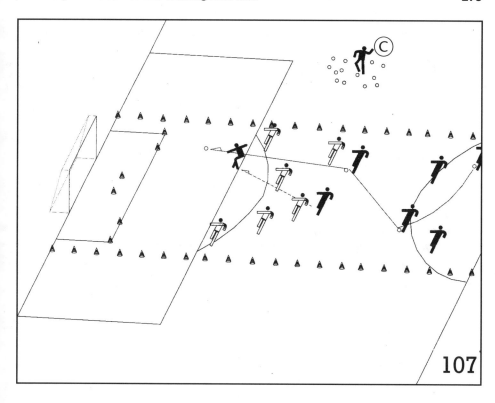

COACHING POINTS

The coach immediately throws the ball into the playing area so that the game is not interrupted.

GAME 108

OBJECTIVE

- Low ground shots with the instep.
- Sudden sprint.
- Concentration.
- Endurance.

This game is a variation of game 107.

The teams are arranged in their respective side and play as in a regular match. One player (A) per team plays near the sideline of his field.

A team scores one point when it scores a goal with a shot from outside the penalty area. Soon after the shot, while the ball is rolling to the six yard area, player A quickly enters the penalty area and tries to prevent the ball from entering his goal.

All the players take turns playing the role of A.

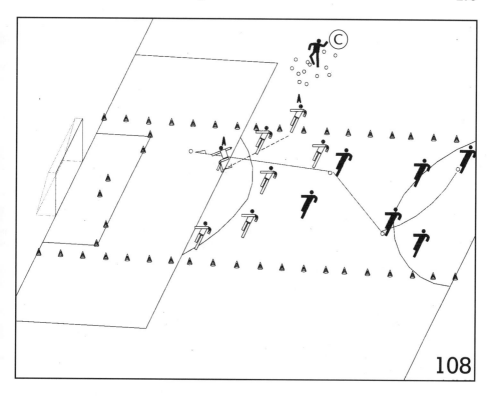

108

COACHING POINTS

The coach immediately throws the ball into the playing area so that the game is not interrupted.

GAME 109

OBJECTIVE

- Shots at goal from outside the penalty area.
- Endurance.
- Concentration.

Team game: played by 2 teams.

The playing area is reduced according to the number of players. Two goals are placed on the goal line, at a distance of 10-15 yards from each other: so each team has its own target.

The coach has several balls and is placed just outside the playing area.

The teams play a match with two balls but with a different goal per team. The shot at goal can be carried out only from outside the penalty area. A goal is valid only if scored into the goal that represents the team's target.

Exactly when a ball is shot the coach immediately throws another ball into the field.

The go is won by the team that has scored more goals once the coach has run out of balls.

After each repetition the teams switch the target goals.

The winner is the team that wins the pre-established number of goes first.

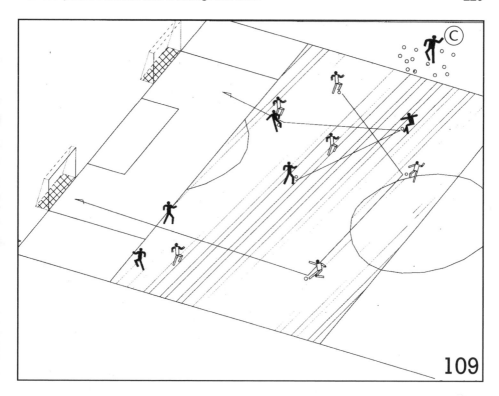

109

COACHING POINTS

This game is very demanding.

If the players are not in a position to play with two balls at the same time the coach waits for some seconds before throwing the next ball.

GAME 110

OBJECTIVE

- Deep penetrating passes at the right time.
- Concentration.
- Speed of action.
- Endurance.

Team game: played by 2 teams.

The playing area is reduced according to the number of players. Two cone-marked small goals are placed on each end line. The field is divided in three parts by using cones. Some players of each team are arranged in the central part and pass the ball to each other; other players defend their six yard area and the attackers play in the opponents' six yard area.

The coach has several balls and is placed just outside the playing area: he gives the starting signal by throwing a ball into the central zone of the field.

The players in that zone try to make a pass to their teammates in the opponents' six yard area, who must score into one of the two small goals. When the defenders win the ball they pass it to their teammates in the center. Exactly when a ball is passed into the six yard area the coach immediately throws another ball into the central zone or into the other six yard area where there is no ball.

To avoid confusion, the coach must make sure that there are no more than two balls in the field.

The go is won by the team that has scored more goals once the coach has run out of balls.

Every now and then the players should switch zones and roles.

The winner is the team that wins the pre-established number of goes first.

110

COACHING POINTS

If the players are not in a position to play with two balls at the same time the coach throws the second ball only after examining the situation of the moment.

GAME 111

OBJECTIVE

- Speed of action.
- Attack with superiority in numbers.
- Speed/Endurance.
- Concentration.
- Shots at goal from outside the penalty area.

Team game: played by 2 teams.
Playing area: the playing area is a smaller field in front of the penalty area, reduced according to the number of players. Just beyond the end line opposite the goal a short circuit is arranged.

One team attacks the goal defended by the opposing team and by a goalkeeper.

The coach has several balls and is just outside the field: he starts the game by throwing a ball into the field.

The players in white attack and try to score a goal without entering the penalty area.

As soon as they shoot at goal the coach immediately throws another ball into the field.

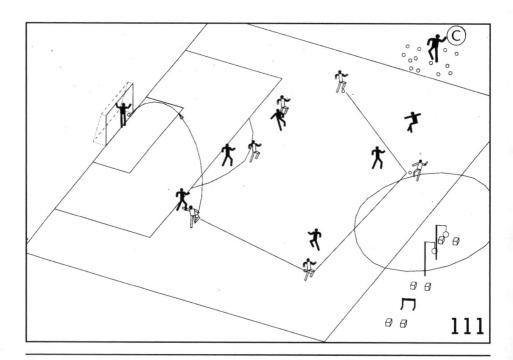

111

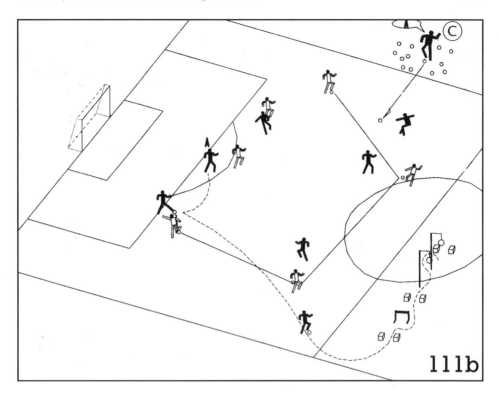

111b

The players in black are the defenders: when they intercept or touch the ball, the coach calls out the name of a defender (A) and throws another ball into the field to let the game continue.

The nominated defender quickly dribbles the intercepted ball through the circuit up to the end. He leaves it there then quickly runs back through the circuit and goes back to the playing area.

Each goal scores a point for the attackers; each ball dribbled to the end of the circuit scores a point for the defenders. The go is won by the team with the higher score once the coach has run out of balls.

After each repetition the teams switch their roles.

The winner is the team that wins the pre-established number of goes first.

COACHING POINTS

Ask the attackers to volley-pass the ball.

GAME 112

OBJECTIVE

- Speed of action.
- Deep penetrating passes.
- Concentration.
- Endurance.

Team game: played by 3 teams (A - B - C: C is made up of 2-3 players).

The playing area has two goals and is reduced according to the number of players.

In the middle of the field mark a central zone and arrange there the players of team C. Place the players of teams A and B into the zones of their respective roles.

The attackers play in the opponents' six yard area; the defenders pass them the ball and defend their six yard area. The coach has several balls and is just outside the field: he starts the game by throwing a ball into either six yard area. Teams A and B defend and attack without entering the central zone. When the defenders pass the ball to their teammates in the attack the players of team C in the central zone try to intercept it. Whether the ball is intercepted by team C or goes beyond the central zone into the six yard area, the coach immediately throws another ball into the six yard area from where the other ball has been passed.

To avoid confusion, the coach must make sure that there are no more than two balls in the field.

The winner is the team that has scored more goals or intercepted more balls once the coach has run out of balls.

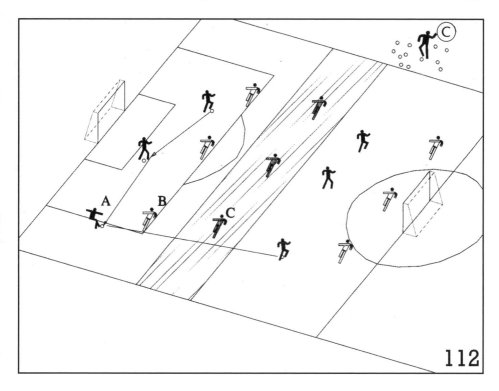

112

COACHING POINTS

The coach throws the second ball only after examining the situation of the moment.

GAME 113

OBJECTIVE

- Deep penetrating passes.
- Playing with inferiority in numbers.
- Deep long passes.
- Speed of performance.
- Endurance.
- Concentration.

This game is a variation of game 112.
Team game: played by 2 teams.
The team in black plays with superiority in numbers: it has one more player in the attack and one more in the defense.

In the central zone there are two players in white who try to intercept the opponents' passes.

The defenders in black must pass the ball across the central zone to their teammates in the attack; the defenders in white make long passes above the central zone to their teammates in the attack.

At the end of each go the teams switch their roles.

Each go is won by the team that scores more goals and intercepts more balls.

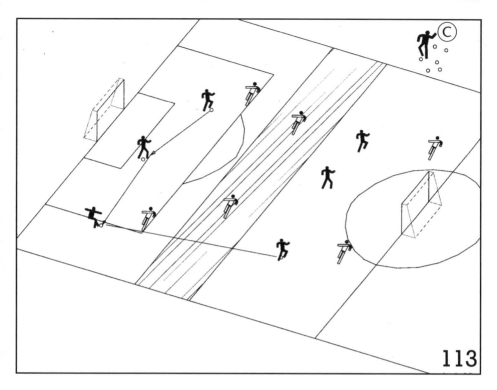

113

COACHING POINTS

The coach throws a second ball into the field so that the game is not interrupted.

GAME 114

OBJECTIVE

- Playing with inferiority in numbers.
- Speed of performance.
- Concentration.
- Endurance.
- Two on two.

This game is a variation of game 113.
In the central zone there are two players for each team.

The players of the two teams must pass the ball across the central zone to their teammates in the attack. When the players in the central zone intercept the ball they play two on two: the player who manages to get out of the zone in possession of the ball becomes an extra attacker.

When the ball is won by the opposing defenders the extra attacker quickly returns to the central zone.

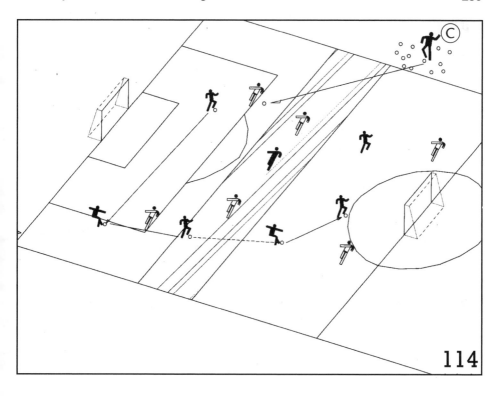

114

COACHING POINTS

Ask the player who gets out of the central zone to dribble the ball along the wings and cross, or to make deep long passes.

The coach throws the next balls only after examining the situation of the moment.

GAME 115

OBJECTIVE

- Defending with inferiority in numbers.
- Speed of performance.
- Endurance.
- Concentration.

This game is a variation of game 114.

There are no players in the central zone: only a defender in possession of the ball can enter it while dribbling and when he does only one opposing attacker can challenge him. If the defender manages to cross the central area and keep possession of the ball he becomes an extra attacker, but as soon as the opponents win the ball he quickly returns to the central zone.

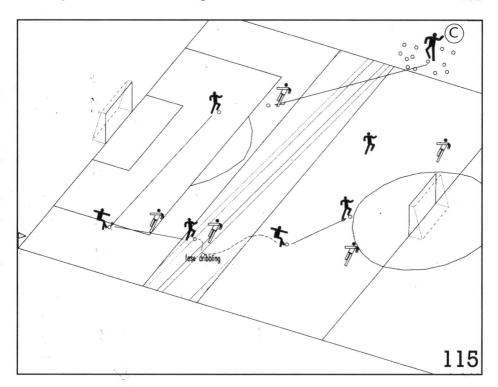

fase dribbling

115

COACHING POINTS

Ask the player who gets out of the central zone to dribble the ball along the wings.

The coach throws the next balls only after examining the situation of the moment.

GAME 116

OBJECTIVE

- Quickness of reflexes.
- Accurate shots.
- Headers.

Team game: played by 2 teams.

The dimensions of the playing area depend on the number of players. The field is divided in two halves by a thick line of flags acting as a net. Put some higher flags (over 2 yards) in between the regular ones in such a way as to form three 2-3 yard wide small goals, as shown in the diagram. The two outer small goals are at a distance of about 8 yards from each other. In each half of the field mark a zone where the players cannot enter to shoot the ball through the small goals: each of these zones stretches for about 10 yards, starting from the line of the flags.

The teams are arranged in the two opposite halves.

When the coach gives the signal the game starts: one player shoots the ball with the instep over the flags.

The opponents shoot the ball back with any part of the body except the hands: by volley, after a bounce or after three passes. A point is scored when the ball goes through one of the three small goals.

The winner is the team that reaches the pre-established score first.

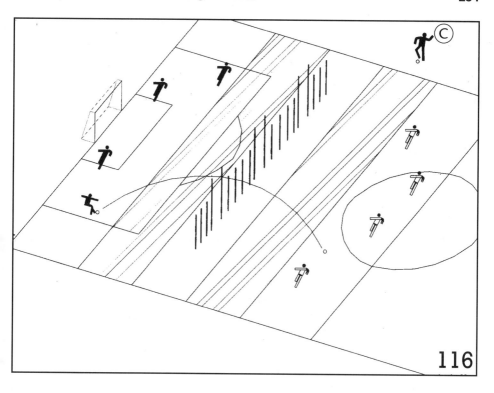

116

COACHING POINTS

This game is suitable also for a gymnasium.
Ask the players not to stand too close to the zone they cannot enter.

GAME 117

OBJECTIVE

- Quickness of reflexes.
- Accurate passes.
- Anticipation.
- Speed.

Team game: played by 2 teams.

The dimensions of the playing area depend on the number of players. The field is divided in two halves by a thick line of flags acting as a volleyball net and there is a circuit beyond each end line. The coach has many balls and is just outside the field.

The teams are arranged in their respective half of the field except for 2 or 3 players (players C) for each team. Players C are arranged in the opponents' half and must intercept the ball.

The coach starts the game by throwing a ball into either half. The teams shoot the ball over the net into the opposing half with any part of the body except the hands, trying to pass it to their teammates C. Each team in possession of the ball has 10 seconds to shoot it into the opposing half of the field: challenged by players C, the players can pass the ball to each other and clear it either by volley-kick or after more than one bounce.

To make the game continue without interruptions, the coach throws another ball into the playing area when opponents C touch the ball (even with the hands), after 10 seconds of possession have passed or if there is a foul: at the same time he calls out the name of a player (not "C") who must quickly intercept that ball, dribble it to the end of his half of the field and leave it there. Then he carries out the circuit and goes back to his former position.

Each ball left at the end of the field scores a point for the opponents. The go is won by the team that has made the opponents leave more balls at the end of their half once the coach has run out of balls.

After each repetition, players C switch roles with their teammates. The winner is the team that reaches the pre-established score first.

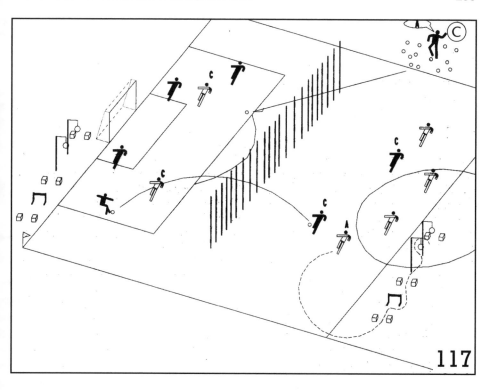

117

COACHING POINTS

This game is suitable also for a gymnasium.
Ask the players to volley-pass the ball.

GAME 118

OBJECTIVE

- Concentration.
- Endurance.

Team game: played by 2 teams.

The field has one goal on each end and its dimensions depend on the number of players. The coach has several balls and is just outside the field. He starts the game by throwing a ball into the field.

The teams are arranged in their respective half of the field and play as in a regular match. If there is a foul, a throw-in, a corner-kick or a shot at goal the coach immediately throws a second ball into the field in order to let the game continue without interruption. At the same time he calls out the name of a player (A) who must quickly run with the first ball and take it to the coach.

The winner is the team that has scored more goals at the end of the game.

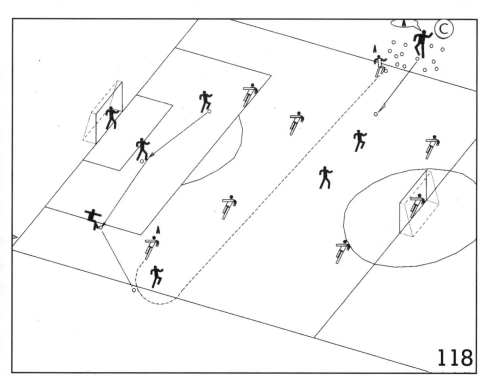

118

COACHING POINTS

If the players are tired the coach throws the second ball after a recovery break.

GAME 119

OBJECTIVE

- Endurance.
- Concentration.
- Speed of performance.
- Playing with inferiority in numbers.

Team game: played by 2 teams.
The field has one goal on each side (four goals: A, B, C, D) and its dimensions depend on the number of players.

The teams try to score into one goal at a time. The coach has several balls and is just outside the field.

The coach starts the game by throwing a ball into the field to goal C: the teams play as in a regular match, except that they defend and try to score only into goal C.

After 3-5 minutes the coach throws a second ball to goal A while calling out the name of a player.

The two teams immediately start to play with this second ball, defending and trying to score into goal A. Meanwhile the nominated player quickly dribbles the ball to the coach, leaves it with the other balls and then goes back into the field.

The game continues like this, defending and trying to score into the goal which the coach has thrown the ball to.

The winner is the team that scores more goals.

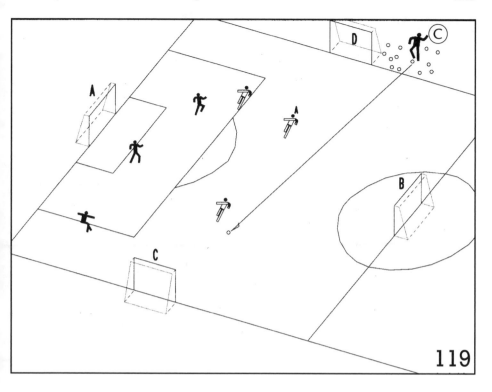

COACHING POINTS

If the players are tired, the coach throws the next ball after a recovery break.

GAME 120

OBJECTIVE

- Quickness of reflexes.
- Endurance.
- Speed of movement.
- Concentration.

This game is a variation of game 119.
After the coach has thrown the ball, each team defends only one goal and attacks the one opposite. When the coach throws the ball to goal A the team in white defends it and tries to score into goal B, while the team in black plays in the opposite way. Likewise, when the coach throws the ball to goal C the team in white defends it from the attacks of the team in black and tries to score into goal D.

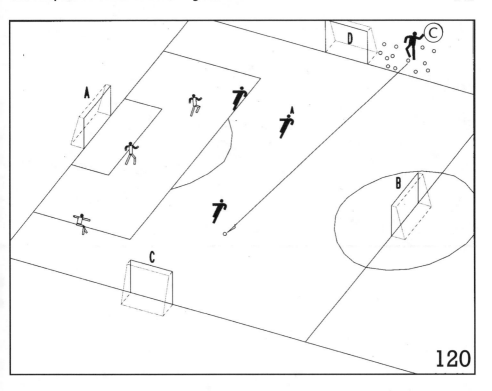

COACHING POINTS

If the players are tired, the coach throws the next ball after a recovery break.

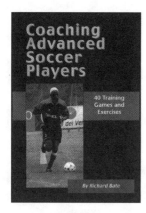
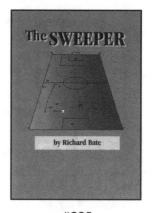

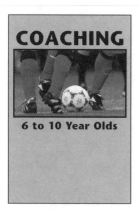
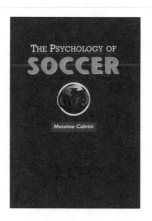
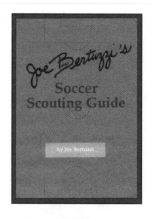

NEW Coaching Books from REEDSWAIN

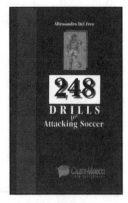

Bestselling Coaching Books

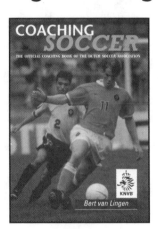

Call REEDSWAIN at 1-800-331-5191

Bestselling Coaching Books

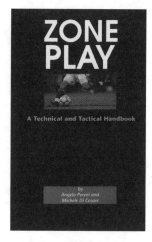

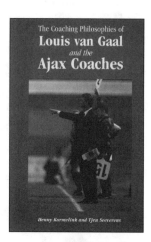
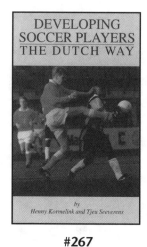